# Head to Toe Science

# Head to Toe Science

*Over 40 Eye-Popping, Spine-Tingling,
Heart-Pounding Activities That Teach Kids
about the Human Body*

**Jim Wiese**

**JOHN WILEY & SONS, INC.**

New York • Chichester • Weinheim • Brisbane • Singapore • Toronto

Published by John Wiley & Sons, Inc.
Published simultaneously in Canada.
Text design and production by Navta Associates, Inc.

The publisher and the author have made every reasonable effort to ensure that the experiments and activities in this book are safe when conducted as instructed but assume no responsibility for any damage caused or sustained while performing the experiments or activities in the book. Parents, guardians, and/or teachers should supervise young readers who undertake the experiments and activities in this book.

*Library of Congress Cataloging-in-Publication Data*
Wiese, Jim
     Head to toe science : over 40 eye-popping, spine-tingling, heart-pounding activities that teach kids about the human body / Jim Wiese.
          p.    cm. — (Jim Wiese science series)
     Summary: Introduces the circulatory system, muscles, digestion, senses, and other body parts and functions through a collection of activities and experiments which can be developed into science fair projects.
     ISBN 0-471-33203-8
     1. Human physiology Juvenile literature. 2. Body, Human Juvenile literature. 3. Science projects Juvenile literature. [1. Human physiology—Experiments. 2. Body, Human—Experiments. 3. Experiments. 4. Science projects.] I. Title. II. Series.
QP37.W48   2000
612—dc21                                                    99-36150

In memory of my parents,

Lewis and Lottie Wiese,

who always supported my interest in science

# Contents

# Introduction

Have you ever looked in the mirror and wondered why you look the way you do or what goes on under your skin? If you've ever asked yourself these questions and others like them but don't know where to begin to find the answers, *Head to Toe Science* is the place to start. *Head to Toe Science* guides you as you investigate your body, from your brain, which controls your every action; your senses, which interact with the world; to your heart, which pumps the blood that carries the necessary nutrients and oxygen to the various parts of your body. *Head to Toe Science* even helps you learn about the DNA that makes each of us so unique. So get ready to learn more about yourself as you perform over 40 fun and exciting activities about science from your head to your toes!

## How to Use This Book

This book is divided into chapters based on the systems in the body: nervous system and senses, circulatory system, muscular system, skeletal system, digestive system, respiratory system, reproductive system, and integumentary system (skin, hair, and nails). In each chapter there are groups of projects that teach you about a specific function within the system. Each project has a list of materials and a procedure to follow. You'll be able to find most of the materials needed around the house or at your neighborhood hardware or grocery store. Some of the projects have a section called "More Fun Stuff to Do" that tells you how to try different variations on the original activity. Explanations are given at the end of each group of activities in the project. Words in **bold** type are defined in the glossary at the back of the book.

## Being a Good Scientist

- Read through the instructions once completely and collect all the equipment you'll need before you start the activity.

- Keep a notebook. Write down what you do in each activity and what happens.

■ Follow the instructions carefully. *Do not attempt to do by yourself any steps that require the help of an adult.*

■ If an activity does not work properly the first time, try again or try doing it in a slightly different way. Experiments don't always work perfectly the first time.

■ Always have an open mind that asks questions and looks for answers. The basis of good science is asking good questions and finding the best answers.

## Increasing Your Understanding

■ Make small changes in the design of the equipment or project to see if the results stay the same. Change only one thing at a time so you can tell which change caused a particular result.

■ Make up an experiment to test your own ideas about how the body works.

■ Look at the world around you for examples of the scientific principles that you have learned.

■ Don't worry if at first you don't understand how the body works. There will always be new things to discover. Remember that many of the most famous discoveries were made by accident.

## Using This Book to Do a Science Fair Project

Many of the activities in this book can serve as the starting point for a science fair project. After you've done the activity as it is written in the book, what questions come to mind? Some possible projects are suggested in the section of the activities called "More Fun Stuff to Do."

To begin your science fair project, first write down the problem you want to study and come up with a hypothesis. A **hypothesis** is an educated guess about the results of an experiment you are going to perform. For example, if you enjoy performing the "I'll Huff and I'll Puff" activity, you may want to find out the lung capacity of other people as well. One possible hypothesis for this experiment could be that the older people are, the larger their lung capacity.

Next you will have to devise an experiment to test your hypothesis. In the "I'll Huff and I'll Puff" example, you might test several people, record their ages, and observe the results. Be sure to keep careful records of your experiment. Next, analyze the data you recorded. In

"I'll Huff and I'll Puff," you could create a table showing the ages and lung capacity of your test subjects or graph the results. Finally, come up with a conclusion that shows how your results prove or disprove your hypothesis.

This process is called the **scientific method.** When following the scientific method, you begin with a hypothesis, test it with an experiment, analyze the results, and draw a conclusion.

## A Word of Warning

Some science activities can be dangerous. *Ask an adult to help you with activities that call for adult help, such as those that involve matches, knives, or other dangerous materials.* Don't forget to ask your parents' permission to use household items, and put away your equipment and clean up your work area when you have finished an activity. Good scientists are careful and avoid accidents.

# Gray Matter

## The Brain and the Nervous System

There are several things that all **organisms** (living things) have in common. One of those characteristics is that they respond to their environment by sensing things that happen in their surroundings and reacting to them. The parts of your body that control your physical reactions to the environment are called the **nervous system.** The nervous system consists of your brain, spinal cord, and nerves. The nervous system is an elaborate communication system that collects information and sends messages throughout your body. Your brain alone contains more than 100 billion nerve cells. **Nerves** are special cells that communicate using electrochemical impulses. An **electrochemical impulse** is a process that uses chemicals to create an electrical impulse. Nerve cells do not touch each other, but meet at a **synapse,** a small gap where the electrochemical impulse releases a chemical messenger that transfers the impulse from one nerve cell to the next.

**Sensory nerves** collect information from your environment such as hot, cold, touch, pressure, and pain. They send this information to your brain, which decides how to react. The **brain** and **spinal cord** are collections of **interneurons,** nerves that link other nerves within the body. Once your brain decides on the appropriate response, it sends messages to other nerves called **motor nerves,** which direct your muscles to move.

Sometimes you respond to what is happening around you and at other times you respond to what is happening inside of you. For instance, you hear a friend call your name and you turn and say hello. A mosquito lands on your skin and again you respond, but this time your response is different. You try to slap the mosquito. When you get hungry, you eat, and so on.

The activities in this chapter will help you investigate how your brain and nervous system keep you in contact with your environment by telling you what is happening and deciding how to act on that information.

# READING RAINBOWS

I'm sure you are a good reader, and that you can easily identify the colors red, blue, and green. But is it possible to confuse your mind so that it mixes up the words and colors that you see? Try this activity to find out.

## Materials

6 different colored felt-tip pens

paper

## Procedure

1. Use the felt-tip pens to make a list of the names of six colors. Write out each color's name with a different colored pen, but don't use the color of pen that matches the name. For example, don't use the green pen to write out the word "GREEN."

2. Read the words on the list out loud as fast as you can.

3. Read the list again, only this time say the color that the word is written in. What happens? Which is easier to do?

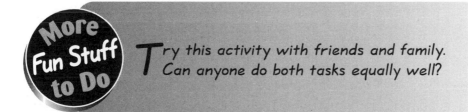

**More Fun Stuff to Do**

Try this activity with friends and family. Can anyone do both tasks equally well?

## Explanation

You should have little trouble reading the words on the page, but you will find it takes longer to say the color that the word is written in.

Different areas of the brain have different responsibilities. For example, the area of the brain responsible for vision is located near the back of your brain, while your knowledge of colors is located in the front of your brain. The area responsible for speaking is located along the left side of your brain, and language understanding is further back along the left side. When you first learned to read, you were taught to speak and read words. For this reason, there are many nerves that connect the areas of your brain responsible for speaking with those responsible for language understanding. You were taught to recognize colors by sight, so you developed connections between the vision area and the color knowledge area of your brain. When you try to see the color of a word that is spelling out a different color, your brain gets confused. It sees both the word and its color, and sends the information to two different parts of the brain. The dominant part of your brain, however, is the part that understands language, so your first impulse is to name the color that the word spells out. It takes a while for you to say what color the word is written in.

## THINK FAST, ACT FASTER

It takes time for your body to react to messages from the brain. But how long does it take? Try this activity to find out.

## Materials

ruler
helper

## Procedure

1. Hold the 12-inch (30-cm) end of the ruler vertically at arm's length as high as possible, with the 1-inch (2.5-cm) end toward the ground.

2. Have a helper stand facing you so that his or her thumb and index finger of one hand are on the sides of the bottom of the ruler. The thumb and index finger should be close to the ruler, but not touching it.

3. Drop the ruler at any time. With his or her hand held steady, your helper should try to catch the ruler as quickly as possible between the thumb and index finger.

4. Calculate the distance the ruler fell before it was caught, using the inch mark covered by your helper's finger.

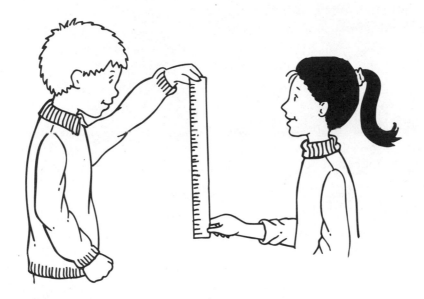

**More Fun Stuff to Do**

*Try the procedure several times. Is it possible to decrease the distance the ruler falls before your helper catches it? Have several friends try the same activity. Do some people have faster reaction times than others?*

## Explanation

The ruler will fall a short distance and your helper will catch it between his thumb and index finger. The distance the ruler falls can be used to determine your helper's reaction time. **Reaction time** is the amount of time it takes for a message to travel from the brain to the muscles in the body and cause a movement.

When the ruler drops, the motor cortex of the brain sends an electrochemical message to the fingers. The **motor cortex** is the area of the brain responsible for creating and sending the messages that cause movement. The message travels along the thick bundles of nerve cells—the spinal cord—that are inside the bones of the spine. Then the message travels to the finger muscles through the smaller bundles of motor nerves that branch from the spinal cord. The finger muscles get the message and close, catching the ruler.

Use the Reaction Time table below to convert the distance the ruler falls into reaction time.

## Reaction Time

| Distance | Time, seconds |
|---|---|
| 2 inches (5 cm) | 0.101 |
| 4 inches (10 cm) | 0.143 |
| 6 inches (15 cm) | 0.175 |
| 8 inches (20 cm) | 0.202 |
| 10 inches (25 cm) | 0.226 |
| 12 inches (30 cm) | 0.247 |

# SCIENCE IN ACTION

In some sports, fast reaction times are very important. Sprinters must react quickly to the start signal. Baseball players also need to be able to react very fast. A good pitcher in the major leagues can throw a ball at a speed of between 90 and 100 miles per hour (144 and 160 km/h). What does that mean to a batter? The ball will take between 0.46 and 0.41 seconds to travel from a pitcher's hand to the plate. If you figure it takes about 0.3 seconds to actually swing, the batter may have only 0.1 to 0.2 seconds to decide when and where to swing and get the message to the arm and hand muscles. It's truly amazing that the human body can perform at this speed.

## PROJECT 3

## TEACH A DOG NEW TRICKS

You have learned a lot of things in your life, such as how to walk and talk, and to read and write. What is the best way to learn a new task? Try this activity to learn more about how the brain learns new things.

## Materials

broom
2-by-12-by-24-inch (5-by-30-by-60-cm) wooden plank
stopwatch or watch with a second hand
helper

## Procedure

**1.** Lay the broom flat on the floor.

**2.** Center the wooden plank across the broom handle so that the longest side of the plank is perpendicular to the handle.

**3.** Have your helper step on the plank so that one foot is placed near each end of the plank.

**4.** Time your helper for 5 minutes while he or she tries to learn to balance the plank on the broom handle so that neither end of the plank is touching the floor.

**5.** After your helper has had 5 minutes to learn to balance, it's your turn. You will also have 5 minutes to learn this new task, but you will spread your 5 minutes out over the day. Practice for 1 minute at a time, then stop for several hours. Your total practice time should be no more than 5 minutes.

**6.** The next day, both you and your helper should try again to balance on the plank. Who has learned to balance better?

## Explanation

You both had the same amount of practice time, but because you spread out your practice over a longer period, you learned to balance better than your helper who tried to learn all at once.

Although no one is exactly sure how the brain learns, the most common theory is that it needs consolidation time to learn a new task well. **Consolidation time** is the time your brain needs to store in a more permanent way the information about how to do a new task. When you first learn a new task, whether it is how to balance on a plank or how to do a new math problem, the information is stored temporarily as an electrical code within the brain. This electrical code is not stable, so you will quickly lose the information when you stop doing the task. However, if the task is practiced over a longer time, the electrical code is changed and stored in a more permanent, stable chemical code. Memory stored as a chemical is remembered better in the long term, which lets you perform the task better the next time you try it.

## LOOK AGAIN

The brain is amazing because it both registers what you see and interprets the information. But sometimes the brain can be fooled into seeing something that isn't there. Try this activity to trick your brain.

## Materials

scissors
Styrofoam plate
helper

## Procedure

**1.** Cut the rim off half the plate.

**2.** Cut the piece of rim approximately in half so you can lay one half over the other.

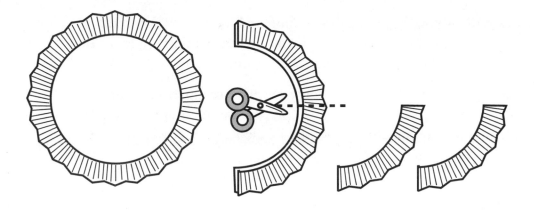

3. Trim the edges of both pieces at the same time to make sure that they are exactly the same length.

4. Place the 2 pieces on the table so that they are facing the same direction.

5. Ask your helper which piece is bigger.

**More Fun Stuff to Do**

There are many illusions similar to the one you just did. For example, which of these lines is longer (not counting the arrow segments)? After you've taken a guess, measure and find out.

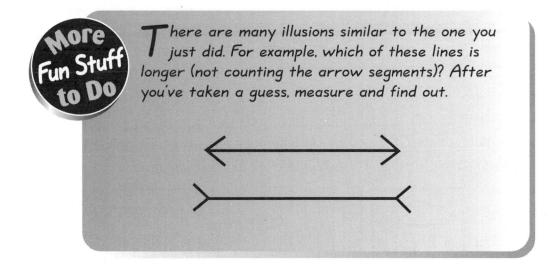

## Explanation

Your helper will have a difficult time telling which piece of the plate rim is larger when indeed both are the same length. Odds are, he or she will think that the left piece of the rim is longer.

There are different reasons for optical illusions. An **optical illusion** is a picture or image that results in a false impression. Some illusions occur when your brain sees something and incorrectly interprets it to be something you've seen before. You assume something looks one way because you have seen something similar before.

Optical illusions also occur when your brain compares two different, but similar, objects. With the plate pieces, the inner arc of the right piece is next to the longer outer arc of the left piece, which makes the right piece seem shorter.

# PROJECT 5 THROUGH THE LOOKING GLASS

Your sense of direction is something that you often take for granted. Up or down and left or right seem easy to tell apart. But what if your sense of direction became mixed up? Try this activity to see how you would react if everything seemed backward.

## Materials

pencil
paper
stopwatch or watch with a second hand
hand mirror
helper

## Procedure

**1.** Make a copy of the two mazes shown below, either using a copy machine or tracing them on another piece of paper.

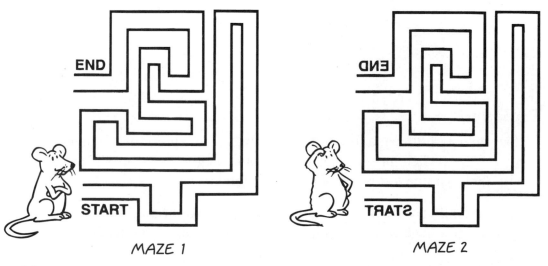

MAZE 1                    MAZE 2

**2.** Draw a path through the first maze without lifting your pencil. Have a helper time how long it takes you to complete the task.

**3.** Have your helper hold the hand mirror so that you can see the second maze in the mirror. Draw a path through the maze while watching the path you make in the mirror. Do not look directly at the paper or pencil. Have your helper time how long it takes you to complete the task this time. Which way of drawing a path through the maze takes less time? Which way is more accurate?

*Try the activity several times. Do you get faster and more accurate with practice? Switch roles and have your helper try the same activity. Is your helper faster or slower than you?*

## Explanation

It will be more difficult and will take longer to draw a line through the maze when you are looking at it in the mirror.

The eyes send a message to the brain, telling it where the pencil is and where the pencil should move next. Over time, your body has learned to coordinate these motions, so when your brain sees that the path goes left, it tells your hand to move left. When you try to draw the maze while looking in the mirror, the task becomes more difficult because everything is backward. Your eyes look at the maze and send a message to your brain, which sees that the pencil mark has to go left. However, your brain knows that the mirror has reversed the image, so it has to tell your hand to move right instead of left. The brain is confused between doing what the eyes are showing it and what it understands it should do.

## STRONG SIGHT

It's easy to figure out which hand is your dominant one. It's usually the hand that you use to write with. But did you know that you also have a dominant eye? Try this activity to find out more.

## Materials

pencil

paper

tape

## Procedure

1. Draw a spot about the size of a quarter on the paper.

2. Tape the paper on a wall.

3. Stand on the opposite side of the room facing the paper.

4. Extend your arms in front of you, palms facing the paper. Make a small peephole between your hands with your thumbs and fingers of each hand.

5. Look at the spot on the paper through the peephole with both eyes open.

6. Without moving your hands or your head, first close your right eye and look for the spot. Then open your right eye and close your left. Which eye still sees the spot?

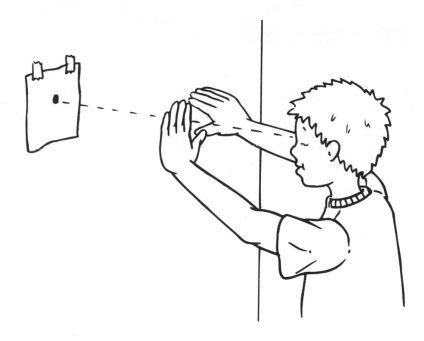

### Explanation

The spot will be seen by only one eye, either the right or the left. The eye you see the spot with is your dominant eye. Your **dominant eye** is your favored eye, which usually sees an object slightly better than your nondominant eye. This isn't related to whether you are right- or left-handed. But in the same way that you have a dominant hand, you also have a dominant eye.

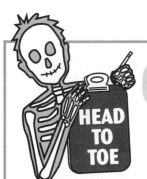

## SCIENCE IN ACTION

Your dominant eye doesn't affect your everyday life too much, but it does affect how you move when you play sports. To allow your body to use its dominant eye more, you will slightly turn your head right or left to let the dominant eye get a better view of what you're looking at. Some coaches have found that a gymnast who has a dominant right eye will make left turns better because the gymnast's head naturally turns that way to let the right eye get a better view. The same applies to a dominant left eye and right turns.

# SPIN LIKE A TOP

Your inner ear helps your body know whether you are right side up or upside down. In other words, it helps you balance. Try this activity to learn more.

## Materials

swivel chair
scarf that can be used as a blindfold
timer or watch that counts seconds
helper

## Procedure

**1.** Place the chair in the center of the room. Make sure you have enough space for the chair to turn in circles without stopping.

**2.** Have your helper sit in the chair, feet off the floor. Use the scarf to blindfold your helper.

**3.** Turn the chair slowly in one direction. Time the turns so that you make one complete turn every 2 to 3 seconds, turning at a constant speed. How does your helper feel after one or two turns?

**4.** After 1 minute, stop turning the chair. How does your helper feel now?

## Explanation

When the chair first begins to spin, your helper should sense the turning motion. After about 30 seconds, however, your helper won't feel the turning at all. After 1 minute, when you stop turning the chair, your helper will feel that he or she is turning in the opposite direction.

Your sense of balance is controlled by granules in two fluid-filled sacs that detect direction up and down and three fluid-filled semicircular canals that detect motion. These loop-shaped structures are located in your inner ear. The **inner ear** contains the semicircular canals along with the cochlea and the auditory nerve. The cochlea and auditory nerve will be discussed later, in chapter 2. The movement of the fluid in the semicircular canals sends messages of movement to your brain. When you turn your helper initially, the fluid in the canals of his or her ears moves. At first the fluid resists movement because of **inertia** (the tendency of an object to remain at rest or continue moving unless acted on by an outside force). Your helper's brain registers movement in the direction of the spin. But as the spinning continues, the fluid flows in the direction of the spin and your helper no longer feels the movement. When the chair stops turning, the fluid resists the stopping motion and incorrectly sends signals to your helper's brain that he or she is turning in the opposite direction.

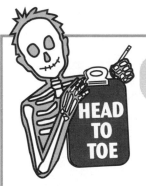

## SCIENCE IN ACTION

Living in space can cause problems with the inner ear's ability to regulate balance. As astronauts orbit Earth, they float around in the space shuttle cabin. This weightlessness affects the inner ear. On Earth, even with your eyes closed, you know which direction is down because gravity pulls down on the granules in the fluid-filled sacs of your inner ear. When astronauts are in orbit, gravity no longer pulls on these granules, so this sense of downward direction is affected. An astronaut's sense of balance is affected much as your helper's was in this activity. When astronauts return to Earth, they can't balance for several hours. Eventually, however, their sense of balance comes back.

# Feel Your Way

## The Senses and the Nervous System

In the last chapter you investigated one important part of the nervous system, the brain. In this chapter, you'll investigate another part of the nervous system: the sensory nerves or your senses.

The sensory nerves supply the brain and spinal cord with information about not only what is happening outside your body but also what is happening inside your body. For example, special sensory nerves in the blood vessels in your neck provide information about the levels of oxygen and carbon dioxide in your blood. Other sensory nerves monitor water concentration in blood and blood pressure.

The most common sensory nerves are associated with your senses of taste, smell, hearing, sight, and touch. Everything that happens around you is sensed and conveyed to the brain by your sensory nerves. The sound of thunder, the chill of a cold day, the smells of food, and the soft touch of your parents are relayed to your brain by your sensory nerves.

The sensory nerves related to your senses are highly specialized to do their job. For example, the sensory nerves responsible for hearing specialize in converting sound into a nerve impulse that is sent to the brain. The sensory nerves responsible for sight specialize in converting light into a nerve impulse that is sent to the brain.

The activities in this chapter will help you investigate how your senses collect and send information to the brain.

## CRYSTAL CLEAR

Your eyes play a very important role in connecting you to your environment. They let you see what is happening around you. But how do your eyes work? Try this activity to learn about how the lens of the eye helps you see.

## Materials

2-inch-square (5-cm-square) piece of wax paper
newspaper
glass
water
straw

## Procedure

1. Place the wax paper over the newspaper. Look at the print on the newspaper. What does it look like?

2. Fill the glass with water.

3. Use the straw to transfer a drop of water from the glass to the wax paper.

4. Look at the printing through the water drop. What does it look like this time?

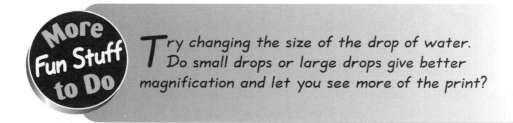

**More Fun Stuff to Do**

Try changing the size of the drop of water. Do small drops or large drops give better magnification and let you see more of the print?

## Explanation

When you first look at the print through the wax paper, the letters are the same size as on the printed page. However, when you look at the same letters through the drop of water, the letters look bigger. The drop acts as a lens to magnify the letters underneath. A **lens** is a piece of glass or other transparent substance with a curved surface that **refracts** or bends and brings together rays of light passing through it. Depending on how the lens is curved, objects viewed through a lens can appear larger or smaller.

All light rays entering your eyes pass through an opening called the **pupil,** the small black spot in the middle of your eye. The colored **iris** around the pupil automatically regulates the amount of light entering your eye to ensure proper vision and to protect the delicate sensory nerves inside the eye. If there is a lot of light, the iris contracts and the pupil becomes smaller. If there is little light, the iris expands and the pupil becomes larger. The **cornea** is a thin, clear disk that covers the eye to protect it.

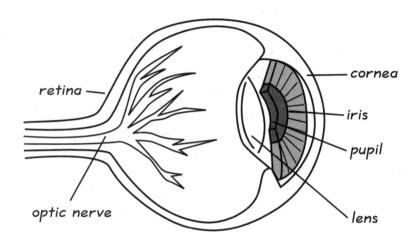

The lens of your eye is just inside your pupil and operates much like a camera lens or magnifying lens. Light rays from the object you are looking at pass through the lens of your eye. Because the lens is curved, light rays going through the top and bottom of the lens are bent more than light rays going through the middle of the lens. In your eye, the lens causes the light rays to meet at the **retina,** which records the image and transfers it to the brain through the **optic nerve** (the nerve that carries visual information as impulses from your eye to your brain). When the image of the object reaches the brain, you see the object.

HEAD TO TOE

## SCIENCE IN ACTION

Tiny muscles attached to the eye's lens change the thickness of the lens to allow you to view objects that are either near or far. A thinner lens allows you to see distant objects, while near objects are best viewed through a thicker lens.

Two common vision problems are nearsightedness and farsightedness. **Nearsightedness,** or **myopia,** occurs when the lens cannot be made thin enough to produce a clear image on the retina. Someone who is nearsighted is able to focus on close objects but has difficulty seeing objects that are far away. **Farsightedness,** or **hyperopia,** occurs when the lens cannot be made thick enough to produce a clear image on the retina. Someone who is farsighted is able to focus on distant objects but has trouble seeing objects that are close. Both nearsightedness and farsightedness can be corrected with glasses or contact lenses. New surgical techniques can also be used to change the shape of the eye's lens to improve vision.

PROJECT 2

## HEAR YE! EAR YE!

Sight is one sense that lets you know what's happening around you. But there is another sense that gives you important information as well. The ringing of a fire alarm, the crash of thunder, and the wind blowing through the leaves of a tree are all examples of sounds you hear. You know that it's your ears that allow you to hear, but how do your ears work? Try this activity to learn more about how you hear.

### Materials

sharp knife

yogurt container

8-by-8-inch (20-by-20-cm) piece of plastic wrap

rubber band

flashlight

adult helper

## Procedure

1. Have the adult helper cut out the bottom of the yogurt container with the knife.

2. Place the plastic wrap over the mouth of the yogurt container. Stretch the plastic wrap tight and secure it with the rubber band.

3. Go into a dark room and stand facing a wall. Hold the bottom end of the yogurt container in front of your mouth.

4. With the flashlight turned on, aim the light toward the plastic wrap covering the mouth of the yogurt container so that the light reflects off the plastic wrap onto the wall. Observe the shape of the reflected light on the wall.

5. Talk into the yogurt container. What happens to the light on the wall?

## Explanation

The light on the wall will **vibrate** (move back and forth very rapidly) when you talk into the yogurt container.

**Sound** is energy that we can hear. Sound happens when an object vibrates and causes the air around it to vibrate. These sound vibrations travel through the air and cause the things they hit to vibrate as well. When the sound vibrations from your voice hit the plastic wrap on the yogurt container, the plastic wrap vibrated. You could see this vibration when you saw the light on the wall move.

Your ear hears sounds by detecting the sound vibrations around you. The ear can be divided into three sections: the outer ear, the middle ear, and the inner ear. The **outer ear** is composed of the outer ear flap or **pinna** (what you commonly call the ear), which collects the sound, and the **ear canal** or **auditory canal,** which connects and directs the sound vibrations to the delicate parts of the ear located inside your head.

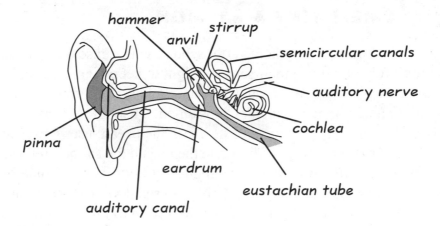

The **middle ear** begins at the eardrum. The **eardrum** moves when sound vibrations hit it, similar to the movement of the plastic wrap on the yogurt container. The vibration of the eardrum causes the three bones of the middle ear to move as well. These bones are called the **hammer,** the **anvil,** and the **stirrup,** named because of their shapes. Because of the bones' shapes and orientation, the vibration is **amplified,** or made louder, as it moves to the inner ear.

The sound vibrations finally reach the cochlea in the inner ear. The **cochlea** is a fluid-filled chamber which contains specialized hair cells that respond to sound waves of different vibrations. Sound information from these cells travels as impulses through the **auditory nerve** to the brain, where the sound is identified.

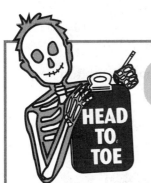

## SCIENCE IN ACTION

Another part of the middle ear is the **eustachian tube,** a tube that connects the middle ear to your mouth and nose. This tube allows the air pressure to be equalized on both sides of your eardrum. Yawning, swallowing, or chewing gum while you undergo pressure changes, such as when you drive into the mountains or fly in a plane, allows the eustachian tube to open and the pressure on both sides of your eardrum to become the same. You often will notice this occurring as your ears "pop."

# SMELL LIKE A SALMON

When you find your way home after school, what sense do you use? Humans rely greatly on their sense of sight to keep them safe and to find their way in the environment. Other animals use different senses to do the same thing. For example, the salmon, a fish that is born in coastal streams but lives most of its life in the ocean, uses its sense of smell. After several years of living in the ocean, the salmon returns to the stream where it was born to reproduce. It finds its way home by using its sense of smell. Try this activity to see if your sense of smell is as good as a salmon's. Could you use your nose to find your way home?

## Materials

cotton balls

something smelly (e.g., perfume, vanilla extract, or crushed garlic)

small paper cup

blindfold

paper towel

yardstick (meterstick)

helper

*NOTE: Ask permission before moving the furniture to perform this project.*

## Procedure

**1.** For this experiment, you will need a large open space. Have your helper help you push the furniture against the walls in a large room.

**2.** Coat several cotton balls in the smelly substance. Place the cotton balls in the paper cup.

**3.** Tell your helper that the purpose of the activity is to act like a "salmon" and try to crawl from the "ocean" (one side of the room) to the salmon's "home stream" (the other side of the room where the smell cup will be located) using only the sense of smell. Your helper will have the first turn as the "salmon."

**4.** Blindfold your helper. Have him or her smell the cup with the cotton balls.

**5.** Place your helper on hands and knees in the "ocean."

6. Put the smell cup on the floor in the "home stream" and place one of the cotton balls on a paper towel on the floor 1 or 2 yards (1 or 2 m) away to help guide the "salmon."

7. Have your helper crawl to the "home stream" by using his or her sense of smell.

8. Now trade places and see if you can find the "home stream."

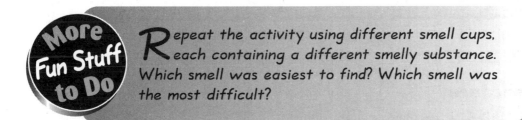

**More Fun Stuff to Do**

Repeat the activity using different smell cups, each containing a different smelly substance. Which smell was easiest to find? Which smell was the most difficult?

## Explanation

You and your helper should be able to find the cup after a little time. While our sense of smell is not as good as some animals', it is still remarkable.

One current theory about how we detect smells is that the shape of the molecule we smell helps us identify the smell. An odor molecule is sniffed into the nose and will fit only into a specifically shaped receptor site in the nose, like a key fits into a lock. Once the odor molecule is fitted into the site in the nose, a message is sent to the brain and we sense a specific smell. Each different shaped receptor site in the nose is specific for a different smell.

The human nose is really an incredible sense organ. It can detect between 2,000 and 4,000 different odors produced by various combinations of the smell receptors in the nose. The sense of smell is strongest at birth and is important in helping a baby recognize its mother before the baby's sense of sight develops. As the baby grows older, the sense of smell will slowly diminish as sight becomes a more dominant sense and the sense of smell is not needed as much.

## TASTES GOOD TO ME

In order for you to taste food, it needs to come in contact with your tongue. But how does your tongue actually taste the food? Try this activity to find out.

## Materials

4 drinking glasses                  unsweetened grapefruit juice
water                               pencil
measuring spoons                    paper
sugar                               cotton-tipped swabs
salt                                glass of water
vinegar

## Procedure

1. Fill 3 of the glasses about one-third full with water. In the first glass, mix 1 tablespoon (15 ml) of sugar. In the second glass, mix 1 tablespoon (15 ml) of salt. In the third glass, mix 1 tablespoon (15 ml) of vinegar. In the fourth glass, place 1 tablespoon (15 ml) of unsweetened grapefruit juice.

2. Draw a large U on a sheet of paper to represent your tongue.

3. Dip a cotton swab into one solution and touch the swab to the tip of your tongue. Can you taste it? How does it taste? On the paper "tongue," record the place on your tongue that you touched and the results of your taste test.

4. Rinse your mouth out with water. Repeat the test, only this time touch the swab to different places on the sides of your tongue. Record the results.

**5.** Repeat steps 3 and 4 with the other solutions, using a new swab for each solution.

**More Fun Stuff to Do**

Try this activity with several helpers. Are everyone's taste tests the same?

## Explanation

Different parts of the tongue are able to sense only one of four basic tastes: sweet, salty, sour, or bitter. The areas of the tongue and the tastes they are sensitive to are shown here.

Humans have about 10,000 taste receptors, called **taste buds.** Our taste buds are located on the small bumps on the surface of the tongue, which are called **papillae.** Each taste bud lasts for less than a week; then it wears out and is replaced by a new one.

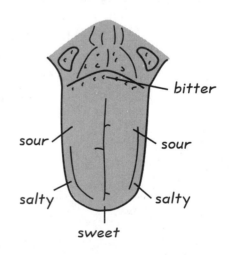

Before you can taste a food, it has to become a liquid. Your mouth does this by adding saliva to your food as you chew it. This liquid helps you both taste your food and start the digestion process, which you will learn about in chapter 3, "You Are What You Eat."

Taste receptors are located on different parts of the body of different animals. For example, octopuses have taste receptors on their tentacles, crayfish have them on their antennae, and some insects have them on their legs.

## SCIENCE IN ACTION

Some people think that if they have to take a bitter-tasting pill, like an aspirin, they would taste its bitterness less if they place it in the back of their mouth where it is easier to swallow. However, this places the bitter pill on the part of the tongue that is most sensitive to the bitter taste. If the pill is placed on the tip of the tongue, it will taste less bitter than if it is placed in the back of the mouth. What do you think is the best way to eat ice cream? We all know that it's best to lick it with the tip of the tongue!

## THAT'S NO APPLE

Have you ever noticed that when you have a cold and your nose is stuffed up, you lose your sense of smell? That makes sense. But have you noticed that you also seem to lose your sense of taste? Try this activity to learn more about how these two senses—smell and taste—are linked.

## Materials

| | |
|---|---|
| potato peeler | onion |
| knife | 12 toothpicks |
| carrot | plate |
| potato | glass of water |
| pear | adult helper |

## Procedure

1. Have an adult helper peel and cut each raw vegetable or fruit into equal bite-size pieces. Put a toothpick into each piece and place the pieces on the plate. You will need two samples of each vegetable or fruit.

2. Have your helper close his or her eyes and use his fingers to firmly close his nose.

3. Use a toothpick to feed one piece of food to your helper. Have him carefully chew the food and try to identify it.

4. After he tells you what he thinks the food is, have him rinse his mouth with water.

5. Repeat steps 3 and 4 for each type of food. Can your helper identify any of the foods?

6. Repeat the activity, but this time have your helper close his eyes but not his nose. How do the results differ?

*T*ry the activity again, but first place a few drops of vanilla extract on your helper's upper lip. Have him close his eyes but not his nose. How does this affect the results of the activity?

## Explanation

When your helper closes his nose, he will have a difficult time identifying the food. When he closes his eyes but not his nose, he should be able to identify the food easily.

Tasting food involves more than just the taste receptors on your tongue. The smell, texture, temperature, and look of food all contribute to how you perceive its taste. The **olfactory nerve** in either side of your nose sends smell information as impulses to your brain. Your brain receives this information before it receives taste information from the taste buds on your tongue. Often you're smelling a food before you can actually taste it.

## RUNNING HOT AND COLD

We all know when things are hot or cold. Or do we? We use our sense of touch to tell if things are hot or cold. But just how reliable is our sense of touch? Try this experiment to find out.

## Materials

| | |
|---|---|
| apron | cold water |
| 3 bowls | lukewarm water |
| hot water | timer |

## Procedure

1. Put the apron on before starting this activity. Fill the 3 bowls, one with hot water (but not too hot!), one with cold water, and one with lukewarm water. Place the bowls in a line, with the hot and cold water on either end and the lukewarm water in the middle.

2. Place one hand in the bowl of hot water and one hand in the bowl of cold water. Leave them there for at least 1 minute. Note how each hand senses the water as hot or cold.

**3.** Place both hands in the bowl of lukewarm water. Note how each hand senses this water as hot or cold.

When your hands have returned to normal temperature, find out how well you can judge whether other objects are hot or cold. Touch various objects in your home. Try a table, a pen, a metal doorknob, an eraser, a book, or any other convenient object in your home. List each item you touch, and next to each, record whether the object feels warmer, the same temperature as, or colder than your hand. What do you think makes objects feel hot or cold?

## Explanation

The hand that was in the hot water will feel the lukewarm water as being cold, while the hand that was in the cold water will feel the lukewarm water as being hot.

It's difficult to judge exactly how hot or cold something is just by touching it. The sensory nerves in the skin cannot detect the exact temperature of an object, but they can signal changes in temperature. These sensory nerves alert you when they sense something getting warmer or cooler than it was previously. When your hand was in the hot water, your sensory nerves adapted to the hot temperature. Then, when you placed that hand in the lukewarm water, your sensory nerves detected the temperature as being cooler than the previous bowl of water, signaling your brain that the water was cold. Likewise, the sensory nerves in your hand that was in the cold water adapted to the cold temperature. When you put your hand in the lukewarm water, your sensory nerves detected that the water was warmer than it had previously felt, and signaled the brain that the water was hot.

Most animals, including humans, can tolerate a wide range of temperatures, but can be harmed by rapid temperature changes. For example, some people have died due to an unexpected plunge into very cold or very hot water. However, if the temperature change occurs over time, less harm occurs.

This ability to adapt to gradually changing temperature is often called the "hot frog" phenomenon. If a frog is placed in a beaker of water above 104°F (40°C), the frog will leap out immediately. However, if the frog is placed in room-temperature water and the water temperature is slowly increased, the frog will remain in the water, even as the temperature increases. The frog's temperature receptors in its skin have time to adjust to the increase in temperature. You may have experienced a similar situation when trying to get into a hot bath. If you get into a warm bath, then slowly add hot water, you don't feel the discomfort of a straight plunge into hot water.

# You Are What You Eat

## The Digestive System

Unlike plants, which make their own food, humans must eat food in order to survive. Food contains nutrients that are first digested in the digestive system, then absorbed and transported by the circulatory system to the cells throughout the body. Once inside the cells, the nutrients supply energy and necessary chemicals, like proteins, fats, vitamins, and minerals, which are needed for proper growth.

The **digestive system** is responsible for breaking down large, complex food molecules into small components that can be absorbed and used by the body. Every part of your body depends on the digestive system for nutrients, but the digestive system needs the other systems of the body as well. The muscles and bones in your mouth help your teeth chew the food, while the circulatory system transports the needed nutrients through the blood to your various body parts.

You'll learn about the circulatory system in chapter 5, and the muscular system in chapter 6. In this chapter, you'll investigate the way the digestive system works.

## TOOTH DETECTIVE

Teeth are a very important part of the digestive process, since most food must be chewed before it can be swallowed. Try this activity to learn more about your teeth.

### Materials

Styrofoam plate
scissors
pen

### Procedure

1. Cut the Styrofoam plate into 6 equal pie pieces.

2. Place 2 of the pieces together, one on top of the other. Cut 1 inch (2.5 cm) from the pointed end of both pieces. Discard the cutoff ends.

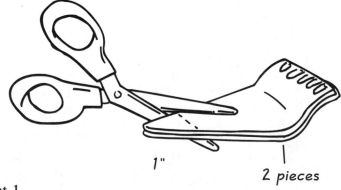

1"

2 pieces

**3.** Put the cut ends of the 2 pieces into your mouth. Push the pieces in as far as possible while still being comfortable.

**4.** Bite down on the pieces firmly and remove them.

**5.** Use the pen to label the upper piece TOP TEETH and the lower BOTTOM TEETH.

**6.** Examine the teeth impressions. How many teeth are there in the top impression? How many teeth are there in the bottom impression? What features of the impressions are useful to tell the top teeth from the bottom teeth? How are the teeth different? Is there anything special about them?

*Collect teeth impressions from several helpers. Be sure to label each person's impressions with his or her name as well as top and bottom. Leave the room. Have one helper take a bite from a piece of cheese or hard chocolate. Can you identify who took the bite by comparing the impressions on the cheese or chocolate to the impressions you collected?*

## Explanation

Your teeth will leave impressions in the Styrofoam plate. Although everyone has the same basic set of teeth, the exact arrangement of each person's teeth is unique. The type and number of teeth, and any missing or crooked teeth, are valuable in determining the identity and age of the person.

Humans have two sets of teeth that appear at different times in life. The first set, called **deciduous teeth,** begins to appear in babies. There are 20 deciduous teeth: 4 incisors, 2 canines, and 4 molars each on the top and bottom of the jaws. The second set, called **permanent teeth,** replaces the deciduous teeth. This process of replacement begins at about age 6, when we lose our front incisor teeth, and continues to about age 18, when we get our third set of molars, commonly called our **wisdom teeth.** We have 32 permanent teeth: 4 incisors, 2 canines,

4 premolars, and 6 molars in each jaw. The incisors and canine teeth are used to cut or tear food, the premolars are used to chew food, and the molars are used to grind food.

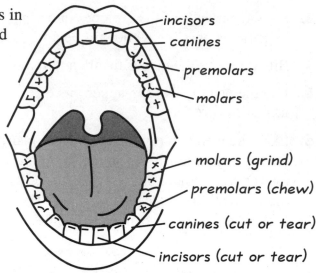

 **HELPFUL SPIT**

The chewed food in your mouth goes through the first stages of digestion before it's even swallowed. Try this experiment to find out how your saliva helps the digestive process along.

## Materials

| | |
|---|---|
| 4 small dishes | eyedropper |
| masking tape | iodine |
| felt-tipped pen | timer |
| 2 soda crackers | |

## Procedure

**1.** Place the dishes on the table. Use the tape and pen to make labels for each dish. The labels should read: UNCHEWED, 30 SECONDS, 5 MINUTES, and 10 MINUTES.

**2.** Place a soda cracker in the UNCHEWED dish. Place a drop of iodine on the cracker. What happens?

**3.** Chew the other cracker for 15 seconds, making sure that it becomes well moistened.

**4.** Place one-third of the chewed cracker in each of the other remaining dishes. Wait 15 seconds. Put a drop of iodine on the cracker in the 30 SECONDS dish. What happens?

**5.** Wait 5 minutes. Place a drop of iodine on the cracker in the 5 MINUTES dish. What happens?

**6.** Wait another 5 minutes, then place a drop of iodine on the cracker in the 10 MINUTES dish. What happens?

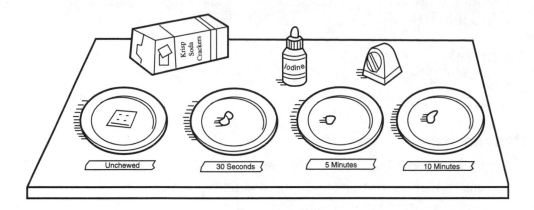

## Explanation

When iodine is placed on the unchewed cracker, the cracker will react by turning dark blue. The chewed crackers will not turn a dark blue when iodine is added. The longer the chewed crackers are left, the lighter the shade of blue until there is no blue color at all in the 10 MINUTES dish. **Iodine** is a chemical that turns dark blue or black when it reacts with starch. **Starch,** which can be found in crackers, is a large molecule made up of many smaller sugar molecules linked together.

When food is put in your mouth and chewed, saliva is secreted from your salivary glands and added to the food. **Saliva** is an enzyme. An **enzyme** is a special chemical that makes chemical reactions happen faster. Saliva's main purpose is to help break down starch molecules, which are very long, into their component parts, the smaller sugar molecules. These smaller sugar molecules are later absorbed in your intestines, where they are used by your cells for energy.

However, saliva takes time to act. In 30 seconds, only a few of the starch molecules in the cracker have been broken down into sugars, so the cracker turns blue. In 5 minutes, more of the starch molecules have been broken down, and by 10 minutes, there is hardly any starch, so no blue color occurs.

# PROJECT 3 — BALANCING APPLES AND ORANGES

To keep all of its systems properly functioning, your body needs a regular supply of water and nutrition in the form of a balanced diet. A balanced diet provides just the right amount of energy to fuel the muscles and to promote cell and tissue growth and proper brain and heart functioning. How balanced is your diet? Try this activity to find out.

## Materials

paper

pencil

## Procedure

1. Make a record of what you eat each day for the next week on the paper. Compare your diet to the recommended daily requirements as shown in the Food Guide Pyramid.

2. At the end of the week, analyze the content of each day's diet. What kinds of foods are you eating? What could you change to improve your diet?

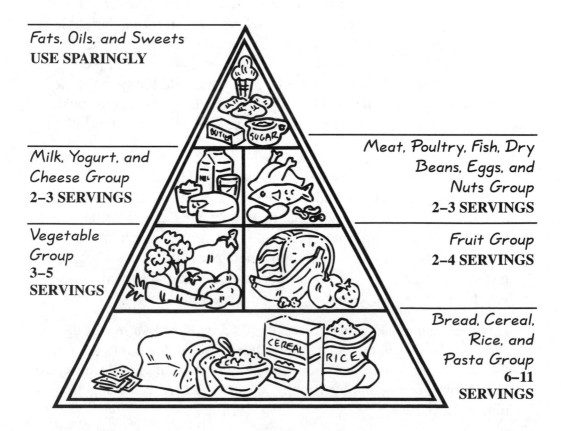

Fats, Oils, and Sweets
**USE SPARINGLY**

Milk, Yogurt, and Cheese Group
**2–3 SERVINGS**

Meat, Poultry, Fish, Dry Beans, Eggs, and Nuts Group
**2–3 SERVINGS**

Vegetable Group
**3–5 SERVINGS**

Fruit Group
**2–4 SERVINGS**

Bread, Cereal, Rice, and Pasta Group
**6–11 SERVINGS**

# Explanation

The amount of food you need every day depends on your age, body size, activity level, and whether you are male or female. To help people plan a healthy diet, scientists have developed the Food Guide Pyramid. This way of grouping foods can help you have a healthy diet if you regularly eat the appropriate number of servings from each group.

The food we eat can be grouped in other ways as well. One way is to look at what each food group does for the body.

■ Protein is needed for growth and repair of cells and tissue. Fish, meat, cheese, nuts, and beans contain protein.

■ Carbohydrates provide energy for the cells in the body. Carbohydrates come in the form of starch and sugar. Sugars are converted quickly to energy, while starches take longer to break down and provide energy for a longer time.

■ Fats and oils keep nerves and other cells healthy. They are also used as extra fuel for the body after carbohydrates have been used up. Fats and oils come from animals and plants. Plant and fish oils are considered healthier than fats that come from animals.

■ Vitamins are necessary to regulate and maintain body functions. For example, vitamin A, which is found in carrots, is necessary for healthy vision. Vitamins are found in fruits and vegetables.

■ Minerals are very important in bone formation and other body systems. Minerals come from fruits and vegetables and other foods, such as milk, which provides calcium for strong bones.

■ Fiber provides roughage, which keeps intestinal waste moving through the digestive system. Fiber is the indigestible part of plant food.

■ Water is essential for cells to function. It carries nutrients and other materials into the cells and takes waste away. It also helps keep your body cool through sweat. In addition to water and other liquids, your body gets water from many food sources.

How does food move through your digestive system? If it only moves down from your mouth because of gravity, what happens when you lie down? Try this activity to find out.

## Materials

scissors
long, thin balloon
measuring spoons
cooking oil
slice of bread

## Procedure

**1.** Cut the end off the balloon so that it makes a long, flexible tube.

**2.** Pour 1 teaspoon (5 ml) of cooking oil into the balloon.

**3.** Take some bread from the center of the slice and make it into a ball about the size of a marble.

**4.** Stick the bread into one end of the balloon.

**5.** Squeeze the balloon behind the ball of bread with one hand. Keeping that hand in place, cross your other hand over the first hand and squeeze the balloon.

**6.** Continue to squeeze, hand over hand. What happens?

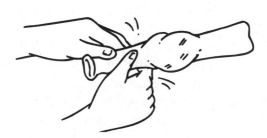

## Explanation

As you squeeze hand over hand, the ball of bread moves slowly along the balloon.

This activity simulates **peristalsis,** the rhythmic, wavelike contractions of the muscles lining the digestive tract that push food through the digestive system. Once swallowed, food travels from the mouth to the stomach by way of a tube called the **esophagus.** The lump of food you swallow is called a **bolus.** The bolus stretches the wall of the esophagus, which triggers the wave-like contractions. This movement continues throughout the entire digestive tract—the esophagus, stomach, small intestine, and large intestine. The movement of the food is aided by **mucus,** a slippery substance that lines the entire digestive tract. The mucus protects the lining of the digestive tract and makes the food move more easily, like the cooking oil in the balloon.

Although it may have felt a little strange, you were able to eat while hanging upside down in the "More Fun Stuff to Do" activity. This is because gravity isn't necessary for food to move from your mouth to your stomach. The wavelike contractions work to move the food along the esophagus whether you're right side up or upside down!

# WHOOPIE WHISTLE

Once the food is in your digestive system and has been broken down into smaller nutrients that can be absorbed by the body, you might think that everything is done. But that isn't always the case. Try this activity to learn more.

## Materials

straw
balloon
tape
scissors

## Procedure

**1.** Place the straw in the opening of the balloon.

**2.** Tape the balloon to the straw.

**3.** Cut the end off the balloon near the middle.

**4.** Blow through the straw. What happens?

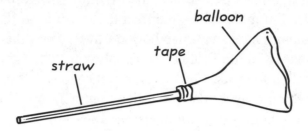

## Explanation

When you blow into the straw, the air will rush out of the balloon and will make a noise similar to breaking wind.

Your large intestines are home to billions of tiny bacteria. Bacteria are one-celled organisms that have no chlorophyll and can be seen only with a microscope. When food enters the intestines, these bacteria help to break the food down by eating the unusable portion, mainly plant fiber. One of the waste products of the bacteria is gas. The gas consists mostly of carbon dioxide, hydrogen, and methane. Occasionally, if you eat certain foods like beans, broccoli, or cabbage, which contain a lot of a chemical called sulfur, then hydrogen sulfide gas is formed. Hydrogen sulfide gas has the odor of rotten eggs.

# Good Air In, Bad Air Out

## The Respiratory System

We live in a sea of air. Nitrogen, oxygen, carbon dioxide, and other gases are taken into our bodies and breathed out with every breath. About 78% of Earth's atmosphere is nitrogen, 21% is oxygen, and less than 1% is carbon dioxide and other gases.

Although the nitrogen in the air appears to have little effect on the body, the second most common component, oxygen, is vital to life. Humans need oxygen to survive. In fact, it is so important to survival that a person can only last a short time without it. By comparison, people can live for many days without water and several weeks without food.

In this chapter, you will investigate the **respiratory system,** the system that lets you breathe.

## I'LL HUFF AND I'LL PUFF

Your lungs are important because they bring oxygen into your body when you inhale and release carbon dioxide when you exhale. But do you know just how much air your lungs can hold? Try this activity to find out.

## Materials

masking tape

1-gallon (4-liter) clean plastic milk jug

water

1-cup (250-ml) measuring cup

felt-tipped marker

washtub

straw

2-foot (60-cm) piece of rubber tube (with an inside diameter the same as the outside diameter of the straw)

## Procedure

**1.** Place a strip of masking tape vertically along one side of the milk jug.

**2.** Calibrate the milk jug by adding water in 2-cup (500-ml) amounts and using the marker to mark off each 2-cup level on the tape. Add enough water to completely fill the jug.

3. Add water to the washtub until it is three-quarters full.

4. Insert the straw into one end of the tubing. Tape the straw and the tube together where they connect.

5. Place one hand over the mouth of the milk jug and the other hand along the side. Quickly turn the jug over and place the mouth of the jug in the tub of water so that the water doesn't come out of the jug. Remove your hand from the mouth and make sure that the water stays in the jug. Continue to hold the jug with your other hand.

6. Slide the free end of the tubing into the mouth of the jug. Note the water level marked on the tape.

7. Take as big a breath as you can and exhale into the straw. Measure the amount of air you can breathe out, using the change in water level on the tape.

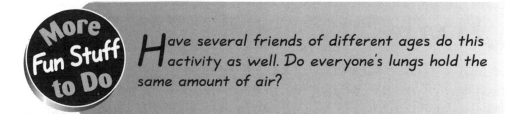

**More Fun Stuff to Do**

Have several friends of different ages do this activity as well. Do everyone's lungs hold the same amount of air?

## Explanation

As you breathe out, the air you exhale forces water out of the jug. The amount of water that is forced out of the jug is equal to the amount of air in your lungs.

Air enters the respiratory system through the nose and mouth. Tiny hairs in the nose act as a filter to trap large particles from the air and keep them from getting in your lungs. The nose also contains mucus, which traps particles and keeps the cells in the nose moist. Air then moves into the **trachea** or **windpipe.** The trachea branches into two **bronchial tubes** that lead to the lungs. In the lungs, the bronchial tubes continue to branch into smaller and smaller tubes called **bronchioles** until they reach small air sacs called **alveoli.** In the alveoli, oxygen from the air is transferred into the blood and carbon dioxide is removed.

A 10-year-old boy or girl has lungs that can hold a maximum of about 10.8 cups (2.7 liters) of air. By comparison, an adult can breathe in a maximum of about 21 cups (5 liters) of air. However, you don't use that total volume very often.

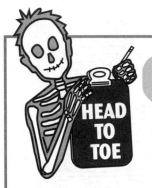

## SCIENCE IN ACTION

The body can store many things. It can store extra food energy in the form of body fat, the liver can hold reserves of some vitamins, and bones can store extra minerals. But no part of the body can store more than a few minutes of oxygen. The human body can survive several weeks without food and several days without water but only minutes without oxygen.

## PROJECT 2 BAG IT

The air you breathe out still has a lot of oxygen in it (about 17%), which is why you can use your breath to revive someone whose breathing has stopped. But it also contains about 4% carbon dioxide. Carbon dioxide is one of the body's waste products. How can you see the carbon dioxide that leaves your body? Try this activity to find out.

## Materials

glass

distilled water

bromothymol blue (found in pet stores. Often used to test water in fish tanks)

straw

timer

## Procedure

1. Fill the glass half full with distilled water.

2. Add a few drops of **bromothymol blue** to the water. The water should turn a light blue color.

3. Place the straw in the water. Take a deep breath and exhale into the straw, causing the air to bubble through the water. *CAUTION: Do not drink the water or inhale through the straw.*

4. Continue to inhale deeply and blow into the straw for 2 minutes. What happens to the color of the water?

5. Try running in place for 5 minutes and then exhaling into the straw. Does the water change color faster?

## Explanation

The water will turn from light blue to green or yellow-green after you have exhaled into the straw for a few minutes. After you have exercised, you will find it easier to change the water's color.

Bromothymol blue is an acid indicator that will turn blue in a basic or neutral solution and green or yellow-green in an acidic solution. A **base** is a substance that tastes bitter and neutralizes acids. An **acid** is a substance that tastes sour and neutralizes bases. A **neutral** solution is neither acidic nor basic. The more acidic the solution, the more yellow the solution will turn. When you exhale, you exhale a waste gas, carbon dioxide. When carbon dioxide mixes with water, it forms a weak acid called **carbonic acid.** This acid turns the bromothymol blue a green or yellow-green color.

When you exercise, your muscle cells use carbohydrates for energy and create carbon dioxide as a waste gas. The carbon dioxide gas is released into your blood, where it is transported to the lungs. It is removed from the blood when you exhale. After you have exercised for 5 minutes, you have more carbon dioxide in your blood and more in the air you exhale. The more carbon dioxide in the air that you exhale, the faster the water will change color when you blow into it.

# ③ AIR CHAMBER

Your lungs do not have any muscles, so how do you breathe in and out? Try the following activity to find out.

## Materials

scissors

2-liter soda bottle (empty and clean)

nail

2 balloons—one large and one small

plastic drinking straw

2 rubber bands

clay

tape

adult helper

## Procedure

**1.** Have your adult helper cut the soda bottle in two about two-thirds of the way from the top. Use the top half for this activity.

**2.** Have your adult helper use the nail to make a hole in the soda bottle cap. The hole in the top should be the same diameter as the straw.

**3.** Cut the end off the larger balloon near the opening.

**4.** Stick the straw in the opening of the smaller balloon. Secure it in place with a rubber band.

**5.** Put the balloon-and-straw device inside the top half of the soda bottle so that the straw sticks out of the bottle opening. Slide the free end of the straw through the hole in the soda cap and screw the cap in place.

**6.** Seal the straw in place with the clay.

**7.** Stretch the larger balloon taut over the bottom opening. Use the other rubber band to hold it in place; then use tape to secure it to the soda bottle.

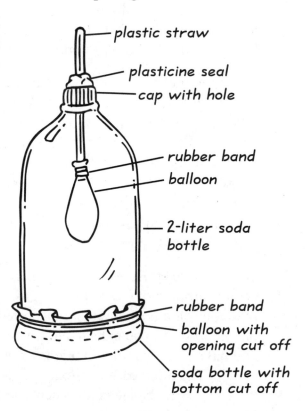

plastic straw

plasticine seal

cap with hole

rubber band

balloon

2-liter soda bottle

rubber band

balloon with opening cut off

soda bottle with bottom cut off

**8.** Hold the neck of the bottle in one hand and pull down on the balloon that covers the bottom with the other hand. What does the balloon inside the bottle do?

## Explanation

When you pull down on the balloon on the bottom, the balloon inside the bottle inflates.

When you inhale, your **diaphragm,** a band of muscles located at the bottom of your chest cavity, contracts. When your diaphragm contracts, it flattens and pulls downward. As it does, the volume of your chest cavity increases and the pressure inside it decreases. The pressure of the air outside your body is greater than the pressure inside the chest cavity, so air rushes in through your mouth and nose. This activity simulates the contraction of the diaphragm (the balloon on the bottom) and the resulting rush of air into the lungs (the balloon inside the bottle). When you exhale, your diaphragm relaxes and returns to its original shape, decreasing the volume and increasing the pressure of air in your chest cavity. This forces air out of your lungs.

# PROJECT 4 CAN'T KEEP IT IN

You can cause some of your muscles, such as the muscles in your legs, to work by voluntarily sending messages to them. Other muscles, like the heart, work automatically without your having to even think about it. The muscles involved in breathing are unusual because they work both ways. Try this activity to see how.

## Materials

stopwatch or watch with a second hand

## Procedure

**1.** Breathe in and out at a normal rate.

**2.** Try to alter the pattern of your breathing by breathing faster or slower. Can you do it?

**3.** Take a deep breath and hold it. Measure the amount of time you can hold your breath. What eventually happens?

*Test several of your friends. Who can hold their breath the longest? Try inhaling and exhaling several times before you hold your breath. Can you hold your breath longer if you do this?*

## Explanation

You can alter your breathing rate voluntarily with little trouble. However, if you try to hold your breath, you will eventually have to take a breath, no matter how hard you try not to. By breathing in and out several times before you hold your breath, you should be able to hold your breath for a longer time. This is possible because you put more oxygen into your blood, so your body doesn't require more oxygen as soon.

Your breathing rate is controlled both voluntarily and involuntarily. There are two sensors located near the large blood vessels that supply blood to the neck. These sensors check the amount of oxygen in the blood that is going to the brain. If the brain is not getting enough oxygen, the sensors will tell the body to breathe faster. When you hold your breath, you decrease the amount of oxygen in your blood as the cells use it all up. When the oxygen level in the blood reaches a certain level, the sensors send out a distress signal and force you to take a breath.

HEAD TO TOE

At very high altitudes, such as those on the top of Mount Everest (29,028 feet or 8,853.5 m), there are fewer oxygen molecules in the air than at sea level. At these altitudes, at first a climber's sensors would cause him (or her) to breathe faster to try to make up for the lower oxygen levels.

But after the climber has been at a high altitude for a few days, his body will have found other ways to help get more oxygen to his body cells. One thing the body does is form more red blood cells. In a recent Everest expedition, the climbers were found to have 66% more red blood cells than normal. Having more red blood cells means the blood can carry more oxygen. The time needed for these changes depends on the altitude. It takes about 2 weeks to adapt to altitudes of up to 7,500 feet (2,300 m) and 1 extra week for each 2,000-foot (610-m) increase in altitude. A rapid increase in altitude can lead to dizziness, fainting, and even death.

Many elite distance runners will train at high altitudes to increase the number of their red blood cells. With more red blood cells, their performance is better when they return to a race at sea level because the increased amount of red blood cells transports more oxygen to their body. After 2 to 3 weeks at sea level, the number of red blood cells returns to normal levels.

PROJECT 5

## MUCUS WHO?

The air that you breathe cannot be inhaled directly into your lungs. It needs to be cleaned first. That's the job of the mucus that lines your nose, throat, and respiratory tract. Try this activity to learn more about mucus.

### Materials

white 3-by-5-inch (7.5-by-12.5-cm) card
butter knife
honey

## Procedure

1. Place the card on the table.

2. Use the knife to spread a thin layer of honey on the card.

3. Place the card on your dresser or other exposed place where it won't get touched. Observe the honey on the card.

4. After 1 week, observe the honey again.

## Explanation

After a week, the honey on the card will have many small particles stuck to it.

The air that we breathe is not very clean. One thing it contains is small particles of dust. When you look at the honey after a week, you can see these small particles stuck to it. The respiratory system needs to clean these dust particles out of the air before it gets into the lungs. The first dirt trap is the hairs in the nose. These trap large particles of dust. Next, the respiratory system is lined with ciliated cells, which produce mucus. The mucus that they produce is sticky, like the honey in this experiment, and dust particles stick to it. Ciliated cells also have small hairs, or **cilia,** that sweep small particles that have stuck to the mucus out of the respiratory system. When you blow your nose, you are getting rid of mucus along with the dust it has collected while in your respiratory system.

Mucus is a clear liquid that also contains special chemicals to kill bacteria that are always present in the air. When you are sick with a cold or other infection, these bacteria are killed and turn your mucus yellow or green.

# Pumping You Full of Nutrients

5

## The Circulatory System

THE HEART

All living things need nutrients to grow and reproduce. The earliest organisms lived in the ocean. These single cells were continually surrounded by seawater. Oxygen and other nutrients in the seawater moved directly from the water into these primitive cells. Once inside, nutrients were carried to all areas of the cell. Waste produced by the cell went out from the cell in a similar way. The surrounding seawater acted as a transport system, bringing in needed oxygen and nutrients and taking away waste and carbon dioxide.

Larger organisms, like humans, use a special transport system called the **circulatory system** to carry nutrients and oxygen to cells and carry waste away. This necessary system has many functions and performs many tasks. It carries chemical messengers from cells in one part of your body to other distant cells, transfers heat throughout the body, helps maintain a proper fluid level, and carries your body's defense against invading organisms.

Whether simple or complex, a circulatory system is important to an organism's survival. In this chapter, you will investigate your body's circulatory system and how it works.

## THE BEAT GOES ON

A stethoscope is a device doctors and nurses use to listen to the sound of your heartbeat. Try this activity to make a stethoscope and use it to learn more about your heart.

## Materials

1 yard (1 m) rubber tubing
funnel
tape
timer or watch with a second hand
helper

## Procedure

**1.** Fit the rubber tubing over the end of the funnel. You may need to use tape if the funnel does not fit tightly in the tube.

**2.** Hold the free end of the tubing next to your ear and place the funnel over your heart. Don't worry if you don't hear anything right away. You may have to move the funnel to several locations on your chest to find the place where the beat is the loudest. Describe the sound you hear. Use the timer to count the number of times your heart beats in 1 minute.

**3.** Listen to your helper's heart by asking him (or her) to hold the funnel against his chest. Does your helper's heart sound the same as yours?

**4.** Ask your helper to run in place for 2 minutes; then listen to his heart again. Count the number of times his heart beats per minute right after the exercise. Count again 5 minutes later. Does your helper's heart sound different after running? Does his heart beat the same number of times per minute after running?

## Explanation

Your helper's heart will beat faster and harder just after exercise than it did while he was resting. His heart will gradually slow back to normal a few minutes after the exercise.

When you exercise, your muscles need more oxygen. To meet this need, your heart will beat faster to increase blood flow, which supplies the muscles with nutrients and oxygen. The amount of the increase in heart rate depends on the type and duration of the exercise. Heavy exercise will cause a greater increase in heart rate than light exercise. The **stroke volume,** the amount of blood the heart pumps with each beat, will also increase. During strenuous exercise, this combination of increased heart rate and increased stroke volume can lead to the heart pumping four times as much blood through the circulatory system compared to when the body is at rest. The circulatory system of elite endurance athletes can increase the amount of blood flow by as much as eight times their resting amounts.

## SCIENCE IN ACTION

The heart and circulatory system can meet the body's blood flow needs during exercise better if a person exercises regularly. Consistent exercise of at least 20 minutes per day, three times a week, can lead to several body changes. With regular exercise, the resting heart rate will decrease and stroke volume will increase. This is because the heart becomes more efficient, pumping more blood with each beat. The muscles of the body also change with regular exercise, becoming able to use more of the oxygen that the blood brings to them.

PROJECT

## ② THUMP, THUMP!

Another way to measure your heart rate is by taking your pulse. Try this activity to learn how to take your pulse.

### Materials

timer or watch with a second hand

### Procedure

**1.** Hold your left hand in front of you with your palm up.

**2.** Place the first three fingertips of your right hand on the inside of your left wrist in the groove below the base of the thumb. You may need to move your hand around slightly before you can feel the pulse.

**3.** Use the timer to count the number of times your heart beats in 1 minute.

Measure your pulse rate at several times during the day—for example, when you first awaken in the morning, during gym class, before a test, when you're watching television, or when you're playing with friends. What happens to your heart rate during the day?

## Explanation

When you feel your pulse, you are feeling blood as it is forced through an artery by the beating of the heart. (**Arteries** are blood vessels that carry blood away from the heart.) This pulse is the rate at which your heart beats.

The heart, blood, and blood vessels make up the circulatory system, which is responsible for distributing hundreds of life-giving substances, such as oxygen and nutrients, throughout the body. Circulation begins with the heart. The heart is a bag of muscle that squeezes itself about once every second, sending blood flowing throughout the body's network of blood vessels.

The heart is actually made up of two pumps. The left side sends blood to the **aorta** (the large blood vessel that leaves the heart) and through arteries, smaller blood vessels, and **capillaries** (the smallest blood vessels in the body) to all the cells in the body. This blood transports oxygen to the cells and picks up carbon dioxide in return. On the return trip, the blood travels in smaller **veins** (blood vessels that carry blood back to the heart) that connect to larger veins and eventually to the **vena cava,** the large vein that leads to the right side of the heart. The right side of the heart pumps the blood up to the lungs, where it takes in a new supply of oxygen and releases carbon dioxide. The blood then makes a quick trip back to the left side of the heart and the cycle begins again.

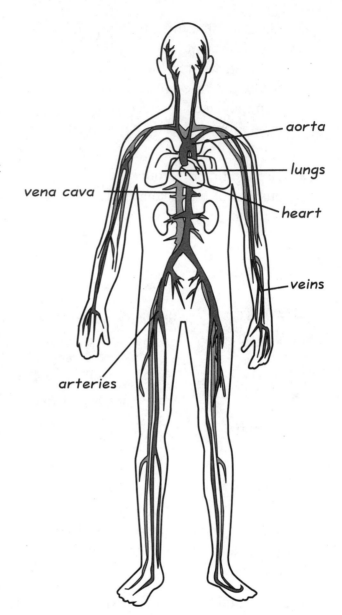

aorta

lungs

vena cava

heart

veins

arteries

HEAD TO TOE

## SCIENCE IN ACTION

If you could lay all the blood vessels in your body end to end, how far do you think they would reach? It may surprise you to learn that they would stretch over 100,000 miles (160,000 km). The blood vessels in your body form an amazing transportation network.

# BLOOD AND GORE

Blood is a very important part of your circulatory system. It contains red blood cells that transport oxygen to the body's cells and carry carbon dioxide away, white blood cells that fight disease, and platelets that clot the blood. They are all suspended in a liquid called plasma. Try this activity to mix up a batch of fake blood.

## Materials

measuring spoons

white corn syrup

cup

water

toothpick

red food coloring

cornstarch

soy sauce

## Procedure

1. Place 2 tablespoons (30 ml) of white corn syrup into the cup.

2. Add 1 tablespoon (15 ml) of water to the cup. Stir with the toothpick.

3. Add 2 drops of red food coloring to the cup. Again stir the mixture with the toothpick.

4. Add a pinch of cornstarch and several drops of soy sauce to the mixture. Again stir the mixture with the toothpick until all substances are completely mixed.

5. Place a small amount of this mixture on the back of your hand. What does it look like?

More
Fun Stuff
to Do

Mix 1 teaspoon (5 ml) of your fake blood mixture with 1 tablespoon (15 ml) of petroleum jelly, using a toothpick. Transfer enough mixture to the back of one of your hands to make a spot the size of a quarter. Tear a circle slightly smaller than the size of a quarter from some tissue paper and place it on the mixture on the back of your hand to cover it. Add another small layer of the mixture to the top of the tissue paper, then sprinkle the area with cocoa powder to cover it. What does the mixture look like? To remove your fake scab, wipe the back of your hand with a paper towel.

## Explanation

The mixture that you made looks a lot like blood. This recipe for fake blood is similar to the one that is used for television and in the movies.

Real blood is a very complicated substance. Blood is over one-half **plasma,** which is the liquid part of blood that is mainly salt water. The remaining part of blood is made up of different kinds of blood cells. About 45% of blood is **red blood cells** that carry oxygen to your body cells and take carbon dioxide away. Less than 1% is **white blood cells** that help your body fight infection and disease. The rest is made up of platelets.

Red blood cells: carry oxygen to cells and carry carbon dioxide away.

White blood cells: fight infection and disease.

Platelets: clot blood to heal cuts.

**Platelets** heal cuts and tears by helping blood clot to form scabs. Trillions of fragile platelets move through the blood vessels. If a platelet strikes a rough surface, such as what would be created by a torn blood vessel in a cut, the platelets break apart and release a chemical that forms thin protein threads. These threads wrap around the damaged area, trapping blood cells and sealing the cut in the skin with a clot. The clot prevents red blood cells from passing through, but allows white blood cells through to get to any infection that might have happened along with the cut.

## SCIENCE IN ACTION

**HEAD TO TOE**

There is no substitute for real human blood. However, there are some substances that can act like certain parts of the blood for a short time. For example, an experimental chemical called synthetic blood is being tested. Experiments have found that when added to the blood, synthetic blood can carry oxygen in a way similar to that of red blood cells. This synthetic blood can be used to replace real blood for a short time if a supply of real blood is unavailable.

When a person needs more blood, such as after an accident or during surgery, the only way to get it is through a blood transfusion. In a **blood transfusion,** blood is removed from one person and given to another. However, the blood must be the right type before it can be transferred from one person to another.

There are four major blood types: A, B, AB, and O. The different types of blood are characterized by **antigens,** or markers, that are found on the red blood cells. Blood type A has the A marker, blood type B has the B marker, blood type AB has both A and B markers, and blood type O has no markers.

When blood is transferred from one person to another, these markers are used by the body to recognize the proper blood for the body. If type A blood is put into a person with type B blood, the body does not recognize the markers on the type A blood. The body sees the wrong blood type as a foreign invader and produces antibodies. An **antibody** is a special protein that is produced in response to a foreign substance in the blood. These antibodies cause the blood to clot, which can kill the person. Because type O blood has no markers, it can be given to anyone without causing any problems. If a person has type AB blood, the blood has both A and B markers and he or she can receive a transfusion of type A, type B, type AB, or type O blood.

## PIPING THE BLOOD

You have learned about how blood carries oxygen and nutrients to cells and carries away carbon dioxide and waste. You have also learned about how the heart pumps your blood. But what about the plumbing that the blood travels through? Try this activity to learn more about the body's blood vessels.

### Materials

light

mirror

magnifying lens

### Procedure

1. Shine the light toward the mirror.

2. Look in the mirror at the underside of your tongue. What do you observe?

3. Pull down the flap of skin just below your eye and observe.

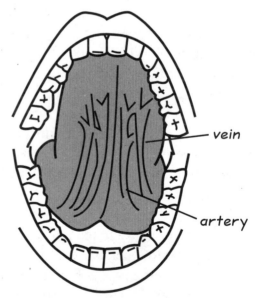

4. Identify lines of different sizes and colors using the following key:

   thick blue lines = veins

   thick pink lines = arteries

   thin lines = capillaries

5. Use the magnifying lens to get a better look at the lines.

ook at other places on your body. Can you find other places where you can observe veins, arteries, or capillaries?

## Explanation

When you look under your tongue and below your eye, you should see thick and thin lines. These are your veins, arteries, and capillaries.

Blood flows from the heart through the body in arteries, capillaries, and veins. Arteries, the blood vessels that carry blood away from the heart, have thick, elastic walls that can stretch with the rush of blood that comes with each heartbeat. You feel this stretch when you take a pulse, as you did in Project 2 of this chapter. After each beat of the heart, the elastic walls of the arteries contract and further pump the blood along its way.

Blood from the main arteries passes through smaller and smaller arteries until it reaches the capillaries. Capillaries, the smallest blood vessels in the body, are composed of a single layer of cells that travels next to the body's cells. In the capillaries, oxygen and nutrients from the blood are transferred from the blood to body cells, while carbon dioxide and other wastes are transferred from the cells to the blood.

Capillaries merge and gradually become larger and larger until they become veins. Veins, which carry blood back to the heart, are thin-walled blood vessels with one-way valves. The one-way valve acts like a door that opens to let blood flow toward the heart but closes to keep blood from flowing in the wrong direction.

# Moving Right Along

6

## The Muscular System

The muscular system works with the skeletal system to help you move. Muscles move bones, which move your body parts so that you can do things like walk and jump.

There are many different types of muscles in your body. Muscles that help you move are called **skeletal muscles.** These muscles help you to lift heavy objects, run, jump, write, and go hiking with your family. They also allow you to smile, frown, or wink. **Smooth muscles** help you to swallow, control the movement of food along your digestive system, and are involved in the operation of your internal organs. **Cardiac muscles** cause your heart to pump blood.

Some muscles, like those that move bones, are controlled consciously and are called **voluntary muscles.** Other muscles, like the muscles of your heart and digestive system, work on their own, without your help, and are called **involuntary muscles.**

In this chapter, you will learn more about the muscles in your body.

# HORSEPOWER

Your muscles help you to do all kinds of things. One thing they do is help you walk and run. Try this activity and see how much work your muscles can do.

## Materials

bathroom scale
pencil
paper
metric ruler

flight of stairs
stopwatch or watch with a second hand
calculator

## Procedure

**1.** Weigh yourself using the bathroom scale. Record your weight, in pounds, on the paper.

**2.** Use the ruler to measure the vertical height of the flight of stairs in meters. You might have to measure the height of one stair and multiply that by the number of stairs you will be climbing. Record the stair height on the paper.

**3.** Use the stopwatch to measure the amount of time it takes you to walk up the stairs. Climb the stairs one at a time without skipping any. Record the time, in seconds, on the paper.

**4.** Use the calculator and the results from steps 1 to 3 to make the following calculations:

**a.** Calculate your weight in newtons. Your weight (in newtons) = your mass (in pounds, from step 1) × 4.45. A **newton** is a unit of force—in this case, the force of gravity that you have to overcome while climbing the stairs.

**b.** Calculate the work you did in walking up the stairs using a unit called the joule. Use this formula: work = your weight in newtons (from step 4a) × distance (the height of the stairs in meters, from step 2).

**c.** Calculate the power, in units called **watts,** that you used to walk up the stairs. Use this formula: power = work in joules (from step 4b) ÷ time to walk up the stairs (in seconds, from step 3).

**d.** Another unit used to measure power is **horsepower.** One unit of horsepower (hp) is equal to 746 watts. Calculate the horsepower used when you walked up the stairs by using this formula: horsepower = watts (from step 4c) ÷ 746.

*R*epeat the activity, but this time run up the stairs. How is the amount of work, power, and horsepower different this time? Can you think of a reason why?

## Explanation

In this activity you walked up a set of stairs and calculated the watts of power your body used to perform the task. For example, if you weigh 70 pounds, and it took you 15 seconds to walk up stairs that were 8 meters high, the results would be as follows: (a) weight in newtons = $70 \times 4.45$ = 311.5 newtons, (b) work done = 311.5 newtons $\times$ 8 = 2,492 joules, (c) power (in watts) = 2,492 joules $\div$ 15 seconds = 166 watts, and (d) power (in horsepower) = $166 \div 746$ = 0.22 horsepower. The average person's body uses about 150 to 200 watts of power climbing a short flight of stairs at a steady rate.

In this activity, you did work by walking up the stairs. You were working against the force of gravity. The work was done by the muscles in your legs and buttocks as they moved your bones and lifted your body up each stair. Most people have about 640 muscles in their bodies. Muscles make up over one-third of your body's weight. The biggest muscles are the **gluteus maximus** muscles in your buttocks, which are connected to the back of your thighs.

## BET YOU CAN'T

There are a lot of things that the muscles in your body can do, but they can't do everything. Try this activity to see that some things that you ask your muscles to do are not as easy as they seem.

### Materials

straight-backed, armless chair

### Procedure

1. Sit in the chair. Keep your back against the back of the chair and your feet flat on the floor.

**2.** Fold your arms across your chest.

**3.** Keeping your feet flat on the floor, your back straight, and your arms crossed, try to stand up.

**A**sk several friends to try this activity. Can anyone do it?

## Explanation

You will not be able to stand up, no matter how hard you try.

In the sitting position, your center of gravity is at the base of your spine. The **center of gravity** is the place where the effect of gravity seems to be concentrated. By trying to stand up with your back straight, you stop the center of gravity from moving to a position over your feet, which are your support base for standing. Human thigh muscles are not strong enough to compensate for the imbalance of the center of gravity produced in this situation, so you remain glued to your seat.

## PROJECT 3 — HAND PUPPET

Muscles do not act alone to make you move. Muscles are attached to bones by means of tendons. Try this activity to learn about tendons.

## Materials

sharp knife

chicken foot (available from a butcher shop)

needle-nose pliers

rubber gloves

adult helper

## Procedure

1. Examine the inside of your left wrist. Rub the area right below your hand. Can you see and feel the cord-like tendons?

2. Have an adult use the knife to cut away the skin around the end of the chicken foot to expose the white, string-like tendons.

3. Wearing rubber gloves, hold the chicken foot in one hand and use the pliers in the other hand to grasp one of the tendons.

4. Slowly pull the tendon. What happens?

5. Grasp another tendon and pull it. What happens this time?

## Explanation

Some of the muscles that bend your fingers are located in your forearm. **Tendons** (strong tissue that connects muscle to bone) run from these muscles, across the inside of your wrist, and out to your fingers. You can feel these when you touch the inside of your wrist. These tendons act similarly to the ones in a chicken foot. When you pull one tendon, the toes in the chicken foot will flex, or bend. When you pull another tendon, the chicken foot will extend, or straighten.

Every bone has at least two muscles attached to it, each on opposite sides of the bone. This is because muscles can do only one of two things—contract or relax. While one muscle contracts and pulls on its tendon, its opposite muscle partner relaxes. To get back to the original position, the opposite muscle contracts and pulls on its tendon while the first muscle relaxes.

## STRETCH IT OUT

Muscles and tendons must be **flexible** (able to bend or stretch) in order to do what they do. Some people's muscles and tendons are more flexible than others, and as a result, they can reach farther or bend lower. Try this activity to learn how flexible you are.

### Materials

carpeted floor

### Procedure

1. Sit on the floor with your legs straight out in front of you.

2. Place your hands on your thighs, keeping your arms straight.

3. As you slowly exhale, bend at the waist, sliding your hands along your legs toward your feet, stretching as far as you can. Can you reach your feet?

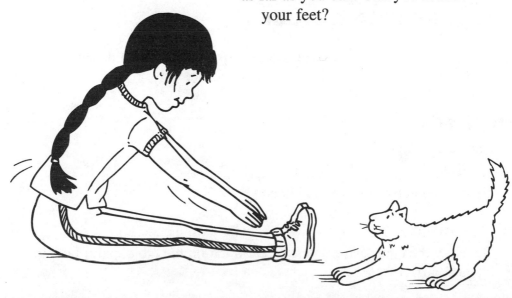

**4.** Practice this activity twice a day, once in the morning and once before bed, for 2 weeks. With each stretch, hold the stretch for a count of 10 before relaxing. Can you reach farther at the end of 2 weeks?

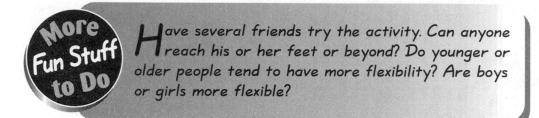

**More Fun Stuff to Do**

Have several friends try the activity. Can anyone reach his or her feet or beyond? Do younger or older people tend to have more flexibility? Are boys or girls more flexible?

## Explanation

Most people have a difficult time reaching their feet when they do this activity for the first time. However, with practice everyone can increase flexibility.

Heavy exercise can cause muscle soreness and tendon damage because of the intense muscle contractions that occur. It is thought that daily stretching, and stretching before and after exercise, warms muscles and connective tissue and increases the flow of oxygen and nutrients to them. This keeps muscles healthy and increases flexibility.

## PROJECT 5 — MUSCLE FATIGUE

Think about the last time you walked up a steep hill. Did your leg muscles get tired? Try this activity to find out why.

## Materials

table and chair

tennis ball

timer or watch with a second hand

## Procedure

**1.** Sit in the chair and lay one forearm flat on the table, palm facing upward.

2. Hold the tennis ball in the palm of the hand on the table. Hold the timer in your other hand.

3. Close your hand around the tennis ball and squeeze as hard as you can, then open your hand.

4. Repeat this action as many times as you can in 30 seconds. Each time, open your hand completely so that the ball rests in your palm, then close it and squeeze the tennis ball.

5. Rest for 30 seconds, then repeat the exercise. Do this four more times. What happens?

**More Fun Stuff to Do**

Try other repetitive activities to see if the result is the same. For example, stand holding a book at your side. Flex your arm and lift the book until it is parallel to the floor. Repeat the action as many times as you can in 30 seconds, pause, and repeat the action as you did in the previous activity.

## Explanation

Your muscles will begin to get tired after you have squeezed the tennis ball many times. Your squeezing will begin to slow down.

In this activity, your forearm muscles become fatigued. **Fatigue** is the tiredness that occurs when a muscle's ability to function decreases because of repeated contractions. When a muscle contracts in order to perform an action over and over, it uses oxygen and nutrients and creates carbon dioxide and other waste chemicals. If the muscle contracts long enough, it will eventually begin to run out of the oxygen and nutrients necessary for the muscle to operate properly. The muscle will also begin to build up excess waste chemicals and carbon dioxide. Both the lack of needed substances and the buildup of excess waste cause the muscle to feel fatigued and to slow down.

# Bony Support

## The Skeletal System

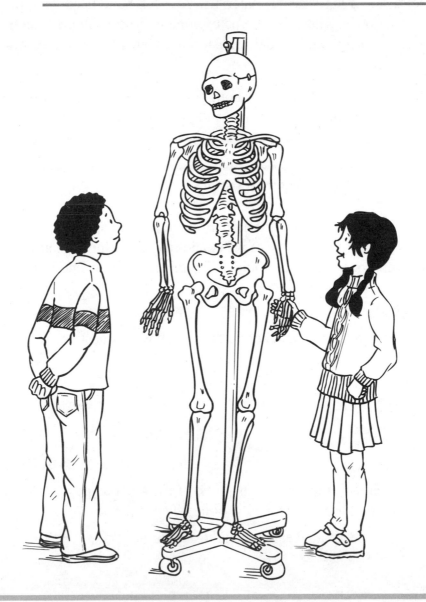

$S$ ome animals, such as insects, have their skeleton for support on the outside of their body. This type of skeleton is called an **exoskeleton.** Other animals, such as humans, have their skeleton for support on the inside of their body. This type of skeleton is called an **endoskeleton.**

The bones in the human body make up the skeletal system. Bones serve several purposes. In addition to giving the body structure, they protect important body parts. For example, the skull protects the brain. The tissue inside bones, the **bone marrow,** makes blood cells and stores fat. Also, bones house nerves and work with the muscles to help us move.

There are two types of bone. One type of bone, **compact bone,** is composed of hard, dense materials. Your leg bone is an example of a compact bone. The second type of bone is **spongy bone,** which is made up of lighter, less dense materials. Your ribs are an example of spongy bone.

There is a lot more to learn about bones. The activities in this chapter will help you investigate bones and your skeletal system.

## BENDABLE BONES

Astronauts who've spent long periods of time in space have found that once back on Earth, they're weak and may even have a hard time standing up. What's the trouble? Try this activity to find out.

## Materials

bone from a cooked chicken (a drumstick works best)
glass jar
white vinegar
tap water
adult helper

## Procedure

1.  Ask an adult to remove as much of the meat as possible from the chicken bone and clean the bone when finished.

2.  Try to bend the cleaned bone. Can you do it?

3. Place the chicken bone in the jar. Pour enough vinegar in the jar to completely cover the chicken bone. (Do not put a lid on the jar.) Set the jar aside for 2 days.

4. Pour the vinegar out of the jar and replace it with the same amount of fresh vinegar. Set the jar aside for 2 more days. Repeat the process every 2 days for a total of 8 days.

5. At the end of 8 days, pour the vinegar out of the jar. Rinse the bone with water and observe it. Can you bend it now?

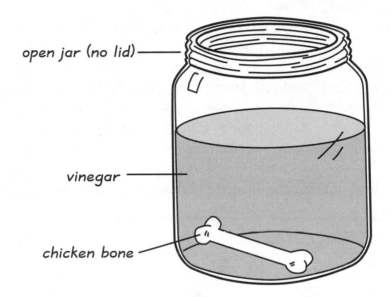

open jar (no lid)

vinegar

chicken bone

## Explanation

You should be able to bend the chicken bone after it has soaked in the vinegar for 8 days.

Vinegar is an acid, a substance that tastes sour and neutralizes bases. In this activity, the vinegar reacts chemically with a substance in the bone called calcium. **Calcium** is an important **mineral** (a nonliving, naturally occurring substance) in the body that makes bones strong. The vinegar dissolves the calcium from the bone, so the bone is no longer strong and you can bend it.

Another way that your bones can lose calcium is through lack of exercise. That's why some astronauts may come back to Earth with weakened bones.

## SCIENCE IN ACTION

Some delicate balances in the human body are upset by the zero-gravity environment in space. On Earth, the body works against gravity every day in actions as simple as standing up and walking around. In response to this work, the body keeps bones strong and muscles fit. But without gravity to work against, such as during long time periods in space, muscles become weak and bones lose mass and calcium. Luckily, the human body does not let bones lose all their calcium like the chicken bone. However, several Russian cosmonauts who spent many months in space returned to Earth after a successful mission to find that their bones were barely strong enough to hold their bodies up. Closer examination showed that their bones were weak from a loss of calcium. The cosmonauts eventually regained their muscle and bone strength after they were back on Earth for a short time. Today, astronauts exercise every day while they're in space to help ensure that their muscles are fit and their bones don't weaken.

## SKELETON MAN

Have you ever wondered what your skeleton looks like? Try making a model of your skeleton in this activity.

### Materials

hole punch

small Styrofoam plate

19 pipe cleaners each 12 inches (30 cm) long

24 wagon wheel noodles

scissors

ruler

12-ounce (375-ml) disposable plastic drinking glass

12 plastic drinking straws

cardboard

pencil

adult helper

## Procedure

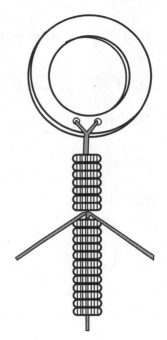

1. Use the hole punch to make two small holes next to each other on the edge of the Styrofoam plate. Thread a pipe cleaner through the holes and twist the end of it so that it is attached to the plate. The plate represents the skull while the pipe cleaner represents the spinal cord.

2. Thread 7 noodles on the pipe cleaner. These represent the 7 **cervical vertebrae** (neck bones) of the spine.

3. Fold another pipe cleaner in half and twist the center around the spinal cord below the noodles so that the ends stick out at right angles from the spinal cord pipe cleaner. This pipe cleaner will be used later for the arms of your skeleton.

4. Thread 12 more noodles on the spinal cord pipe cleaner. These represent the 12 **thoracic vertebrae** (upper back bones) of the spine.

5. Attach a pipe cleaner to one side of each thoracic vertebra noodle. Loop the pipe cleaner in front of the vertebra and attach the other end to the opposite side of the vertebra. Cut the pipe cleaners to different lengths, so that the loops increase in size. The top pipe cleaner loop should be the shortest and the bottom one should be the longest. These pipe cleaners represent the **ribs,** the bones that enclose the chest cavity.

6. Thread 5 more noodles on the spinal cord pipe cleaner. These represent the 5 **lumbar vertebrae** (lower back bones) of the spine.

7. Have your adult helper cut the top ¾ inch (2 cm) off the plastic drinking glass to make a cylinder. This represents the **pelvis,** the bones that make up the hips.

8. Use the hole punch to punch three holes near the top edge of the cylinder, spacing them equally around the cylinder.

9. Loop the spinal cord pipe cleaner through one of the holes and twist it so that it is tightly secured to the cylinder.

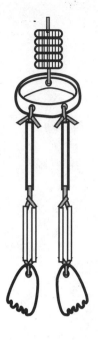

**10.** Cut a pipe cleaner in half and attach one half to each of the remaining holes in the cylinder. Cut 2 pieces of plastic straw, each 4 inches (10 cm) long. Slide the straws onto the pipe cleaners. Make a hook at the end of each pipe cleaner to hold the straw in place. These straws represent the **femur,** the upper leg bone.

**11.** Fold a pipe cleaner in half and twist the center around the hook of one of the pipe cleaners in step 10. Cut 2 pieces of straw, each 3½ inches (9 cm) long. Slide the straws onto the two ends of the pipe cleaners and twist the ends so that the straws stay in place. These straws represent the lower leg bones, the **tibia** and **fibula.** Repeat for the other leg.

**12.** Return to the 2 pipe cleaners you attached in step 3 and follow a process similar to making the legs. Cut 2 pieces of plastic straw, each 4 inches (10 cm) long. Slide the straws onto the pipe cleaners. Make a hook at the end of each pipe cleaner to hold the straw in place. These straws represent the **humerus,** the upper arm bone.

**13.** Fold a pipe cleaner in half and twist the center around the hook of one of the pipe cleaners in step 12. Cut 2 pieces of straw, each 3½ inches (9 cm) long. Slide the straws onto the two ends of the pipe cleaners and twist the ends so that the straws stay in place. These straws represent the lower arm bones, the **radius** and **ulna.** Repeat for the other arm.

**14.** Cut hands and feet for your skeleton out of the cardboard. Punch holes into them and attach them. Use the pencil to draw a face on your skeleton.

## Explanation

Your model should look like a real skeleton.

Your body is made up of 206 bones that vary in shape and structure. The majority of these bones are in your hands and feet. This gives these parts of your body the greatest diversity of movement. Compare the skeleton model you made with the diagram shown. Can you find each bone?

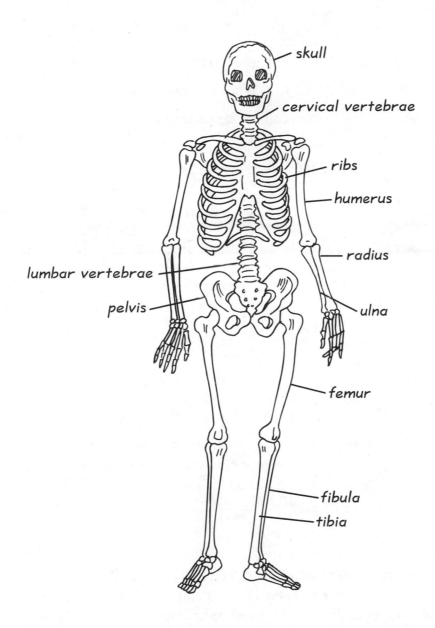

## 3 BONY BLOCKS

Have you ever wondered why bones are so strong? Try this activity to find out.

### Materials

2 toilet paper rolls

heavy book

### Procedure

1. Place one toilet paper roll on the table so that it lies on its side.

2. Place the book on top of the roll. What happens?

3. Place the second toilet paper roll on the table, but this time set it so it stands on end.

4. Place the book on top of the roll. What happens?

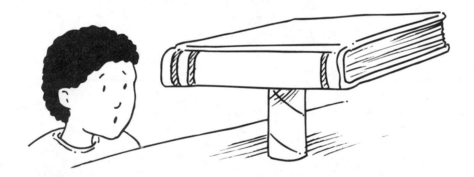

 **More Fun Stuff to Do**

Set a second book on top of the toilet paper roll when it is placed on end. What happens? How many books can the toilet paper roll hold before it bends or breaks?

### Explanation

When the toilet paper roll is set on its side, the book will easily crush it. But when the toilet paper roll stands on its end, it will be able to hold the book with ease. In fact, it should be able to hold several books before it bends or breaks.

Most bones are not solid, but are hollow tubes like the toilet paper roll. A hollow tube is almost as strong and yet weighs significantly less than a solid rod of the same size. This structure is often used when it is necessary to hold forces pushing on both ends, such as in a bicycle frame or the bones of your legs. Gravity pushes down on both ends of your leg bones.

To make these strong, hollow tubes, the outside of a bone is compact bone. Bone develops from fibrous tissue called **cartilage.** As the bone develops and grows, minerals such as calcium and phosphorus are deposited in the cartilage. These chemicals give the bone its strength. The inside of the bone contains other things, such as nerves, fats, or bone marrow, where blood cells are made. The insides of bones do not add strength to the bone.

## A BONE TO PICK

You probably already know what bones look like from the outside. But what do they look like on the inside? Try this activity to find out.

### Materials

leg bone of a cow (available from a butcher shop)
baking dish
magnifying lens
sharpened pencil

### Procedure

1. In the meat department of a supermarket or a butcher shop, have the butcher saw the upper leg bone of a cow in half lengthwise. Have the leg wrapped and bring it home.

2. Unwrap the two halves of the bone and place them in the baking dish.

3. Observe the different parts of the bone with the magnifying lens.

4. Use the point of the pencil to poke at various parts of the leg bone. Which parts are hard? Are there any parts that are soft?

## Explanation

Although we often think that a bone is a solid structure, you will be able to see that it is made up of many different types of material. Some parts of the bone are hard while other parts are very soft. Parts will look very different when examined with a magnifying lens.

The bones in your legs, and in the legs of the cow, are made of both compact bone and spongy bone. Compact bone, on the outside of the bone, runs the length of the bone and is made of hard, dense material. It surrounds a central cavity that is filled with yellow bone marrow. Bone marrow is a soft tissue that is found in the central cavity of long bones, like those in the leg. At each end of the bone is spongy bone, which contains red bone marrow. Blood cells are manufactured in the red bone marrow. The entire bone is covered by a thin covering called the **periosteum,** which contains blood vessels, nerves, and bone-forming cells.

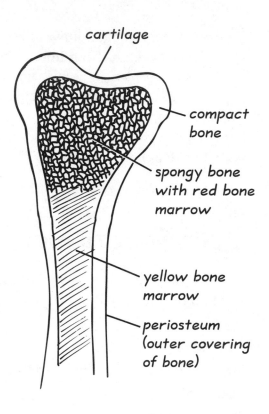

Each end of the bone is covered with a cap made of cartilage. The cartilage covers the part of the bone where there is a joint. A **joint** is a place where two or more bones come together. The cartilage is white in color, is slippery and smooth, and enables bones to move without rubbing together.

## FEET AND . . . FEET?

If someone asks you how tall you are, you might give them the answer by telling them your height in feet. But your actual feet have another link to height. Try this activity to see how they are related.

## Materials

tape measure

pencil

paper

calculator

several friends or family members (This activity works best if you use
   older people who have stopped growing rather than young children.)

## Procedure

1. Use the tape measure to measure the height of each person in
   inches (cm). Write the person's name and height on the paper.

2. Next, carefully measure the length of each person's left foot in
   inches (cm). Write that information next to each person's name and
   height.

3. Use the calculator to divide the length of a person's left foot by
   his (or her) height, then multiply the result by 100. For example,
   if the person is 63 inches (160 cm) tall and his left foot is 9½
   inches (24 cm) long, the result would be 9½ inches ÷ 63 inches
   (24 cm ÷ 160 cm) × 100 = 15. This means that the foot's length
   is about 15% of the person's height.

4. How do your results for different people turn out?

Ask a helper to measure the distance from the tip of the middle finger on one hand to the tip of the middle finger on the other when your arms are stretched out sideways as far as they can go. Compare that distance to your height. Take measurements of different people. What do you notice? Try this with other parts of the body and compare their measurements to people's height. For example, can you use the length of the arm or the index finger to tell how tall a person is?

## Explanation

The length of anyone's foot is approximately 15% of his or her height. If scientists had to identify a person using only the bones of the foot, they could approximate the height of that individual using this technique.

Your bones grow at certain rates and usually in proportion to one another. In an adult, the proportion of one bone to another is fairly constant. For example, as you saw in this activity, your feet are approximately 15% of your height. However, this is only an average. A person's feet can be slightly larger or smaller than average and still be normal. As a person grows, it is not unusual for one set of bones to grow faster than another. For example, a person's feet can be the first to grow, with height catching up a few years later.

# Making You Who You Are

## The Reproductive System

THE FAMILY

Have you ever been able to recognize cousins you have never seen before? It may have been because they share common family traits. Often physical characteristics such as red hair, high cheekbones, or a prominent nose can be traced through a family tree. They are all part of **genetics,** which is the study of heredity, the passing of traits from parents to children.

Your biological traits are controlled by genes. A **gene** is a part of a chromosome that produces a specific trait in an individual. Chromosomes are found in the nucleus of every cell in your body. Because you inherit exactly half of your chromosomes from your mother and half from your father, your traits are the result of the interactions of the genes of both parents. Although you contain genetic information from each parent, your genes and traits are uniquely your own.

The reproductive system ensures the survival of the human species. Human reproduction involves the joining of male and female sex cells from parents to create new gene combinations in their children. In this chapter you will learn more about genetics and what makes you so special.

## MAKING A NEW YOU

You may have noticed that you have some features that look like your mother's and other features that look like your father's. How does that happen? Try this activity to learn more about how you were made.

### Materials

clay or plasticine (two different colors)
butter knife

### Procedure

**1.** Make 2 marble-size balls, one of each color of clay.

**2.** Cut each ball exactly in half using the knife.

**3.** Take a half-ball of clay and roll it into a smaller ball. Set it aside.

4. Take a different colored half-ball of clay and flatten it. Use this clay to cover the first ball so that none of the small clay ball shows through. Observe the new ball.

5. Take the other two half-balls of clay and mix them together for about a minute.

6. Roll the mixed clay into a ball. Observe this ball.

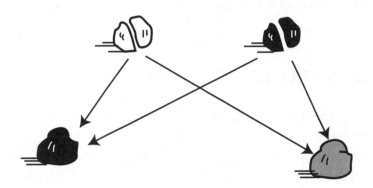

## Explanation

You began with 2 clay balls, each a different color. From those you created 2 balls that each include two different colors. In one of those balls, you only see one of the colors represented. In the other ball, you see a blend of both colors.

This activity represents the way that you were made. Like the new balls of clay that came from the original balls, half of the information to make you came from a male reproductive cell, the **sperm,** from your father, and half of the information to make you came from a female reproductive cell, the **egg,** from your mother. When an egg and a sperm come together to start a new organism in the process called **fertilization,** a special cell forms called a **zygote.** The zygote gets half the information to form a new person from each parent. The cell divides many times and uses this information to eventually form a new person.

Your biological traits are controlled by the genes that you get from each of your parents. In some cases, a certain gene from one parent is **dominant** and will become a more obvious part of your features, while the same gene from the other parent is **recessive** and may not show up at all. In some cases, the dominant gene will completely mask the recessive gene and only the dominant gene will be seen, like the first combined ball of clay. In other cases, the genes from each parent will mix and the outcome will be a blend like the second mixed ball of clay. Some of the traits that make you will be a blend of characteristics from each of your parents.

You actually have over 100,000 genes that combine to make you who you are. Because there are so many different ways to combine the genes from each of your parents, you may look similar to your brothers and sisters, but each of you is unique, even within your own family.

## CHARACTERISTIC PAIRS

How does your genetic information differ from that of a dog, rabbit, or head of cabbage? One way humans differ is that we have a different number of chromosomes than other organisms. The information on our chromosomes is also different. In this activity, you'll investigate chromosomes and how they pass information on.

### Materials

scissors                          paper
ruler                             2 paper clips
red yarn                          pencil
blue yarn

### Procedure

1. Cut a piece of red yarn about 4 inches (10 cm) long. Cut an identical piece of blue yarn. These pieces of yarn represent two chromosomes.

2. Place the paper horizontally on a table. Place the pieces of yarn near the center of the paper. Observe the yarn and paper. The paper represents a cell and the yarn represents the cell's chromosomes.

3. Cut an identical piece of red yarn and place it next to the first piece of red yarn. Connect the 2 pieces of red yarn near their centers, using a paper clip. Repeat the process for the blue yarn.

4. Move the connected yarn pieces to the center of the paper so that they are aimed end to end.

5. Remove the paper clips from each yarn pair and place one piece of each color of yarn near each end of the paper.

6. Draw a vertical line down the center of the paper. How does each half of the paper compare to the paper in step 2?

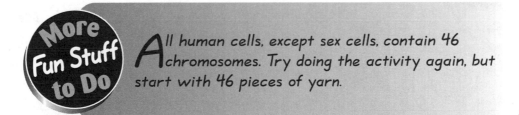

**More Fun Stuff to Do**

All human cells, except sex cells, contain 46 chromosomes. Try doing the activity again, but start with 46 pieces of yarn.

## Explanation

At the end of this project, each half of the paper looks like the paper and yarn after the second step. This project represents how a cell duplicates itself in order to create a new organism. After a cell reproduces, each new cell will be an exact duplicate of the original with identical chromosomes.

A look into one of your cells reveals 46 (23 pairs) chromosomes. The chromosomes are made of **DNA, deoxyribonucleic acid.** DNA is a very special chemical because it is the only known chemical that can reproduce itself. When it is time for a cell to divide, the cell first duplicates its chromosomes, with the chromosomes held together. The paired chromosomes then line up near the center of the cell. The cell then pulls one chromosome of each pair to the end of the cell and forms a barrier to divide the cell into two identical cells.

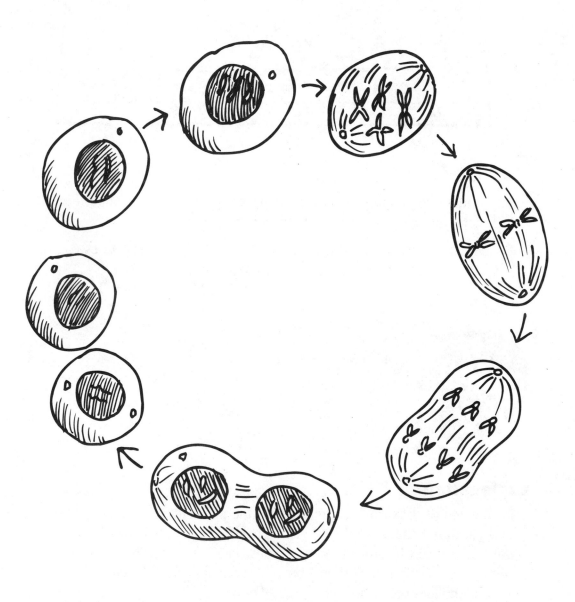

# DNA = UNIQUE

**PROJECT 3**

All chromosomes are made of the same chemical, deoxyribonucleic acid or DNA. DNA is the chemical found in the nucleus of every cell and contains coded genetic information. This coded information determines your hair color, skin color, height, and over 100,000 different things about you, using only four symbols. But how is it possible to create over 100,000 different coded messages with so few symbols? Try this activity to find out.

## Materials

pencil

paper

## Procedure

**1.** Write out the following coded message on the paper:

A G T A C G G G G T C G G A C G A T A C T C A G A C G

**2.** Draw a vertical line after every third letter. This divides the letters into nine groups of three letters.

**3.** Translate each three-letter sequence using the following code:

| | | | |
|---|---|---|---|
| ACT = A | ATC = T | GGG = O | CAG = I |
| AGT = B | TCA = D | TCG = W | GAC = N |
| AAA = C | CCC = P | TTC = X | GAT = H |
| ACG = R | AAA = S | CAT = E | |

What does the message say?

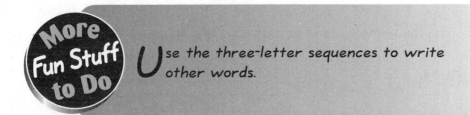

**More Fun Stuff to Do**

Use the three-letter sequences to write other words.

## Explanation

The translation of the coded message is BROWN HAIR.

This activity simulates how messages are contained in DNA. DNA uses a sequence of chemicals called **nucleic acids** to make genes. The order of these chemicals acts like a message to determine your traits. There are only four nucleic acids: adenine (A), guanine (G), thymine (T), and cytosine (C). Each chromosome contains a long sequence of these four nucleic acids, represented by letters. Three letters in a row on a DNA strand form a **codon,** a code for a different chemical. In our simulation, they represented a letter. The chemicals from these codons link together to form one gene or trait. In our simulation, the message would account for brown hair.

The DNA molecule has a very special shape, which was discovered by scientists James Watson (1928—   ) and Francis Crick (1916—   ). DNA is most often described as a double helix and closely resembles a twisted ladder with the nucleic acids forming the rungs, or steps, of the ladder.

# PROJECT 4 — THAT'S ME

All humans are similar, but no two people are exactly the same. Try this activity to see some of the things that make you unique.

## Materials

pencil

paper

parents

## Procedure

**1.** Make a list of the traits you have from the following list. Next to each, write the appropriate letter—D for a dominant trait or R for a recessive trait.

■ Hair—dark (D) or light (R)

■ Eyes—dark, hazel, or green (D) or blue or gray (R)

- Nose—turned up (D) or turned down (R)

- Dimples—yes (D) or no (R)

- Hair on middle joints of fingers—yes (D) or no (R)

- Freckles—yes (D) or no (R)

- Earlobes—free (D) or attached (R)

- Handed—right (D) or left (R)

2. Make the same list for your mother and/or father, if possible. Compare their lists to yours. Do you get more traits from one parent? Do you inherit more dominant traits or recessive traits?

*There are other special traits that can also be inherited. Can you roll your tongue into a lengthwise tube? When you clasp your hands, is the right thumb or left thumb on top? Can you bend the top joint of your finger without bending the other joints?*

## Explanation

Every person is a mix of traits that are received from both parents. These traits are instructions carried on genes, which are found on chromosomes. Each trait comes from two genes, one from the father and one from the mother. Some traits are dominant while others are recessive. A dominant trait is one that shows itself if two different traits are present, while a recessive trait is one that doesn't. For example, if your father has free earlobes, a dominant trait, and your mother has attached earlobes, a recessive trait, chances are you will have free earlobes.

Since there are at least two genes for each trait, it's not always possible to determine whether a person carries two dominant genes for the trait or one dominant and one recessive. Each will show itself in the same way.

## SCIENCE IN ACTION

The person who first studied genetics scientifically was an Austrian monk named Gregor Mendel (1822–1884). Mendel worked with garden peas, studying flower color, seed shape and color, pod shape and color, flower position, and stem length. By studying how these traits were passed from one generation of plant to the next, he provided the basis for understanding heredity.

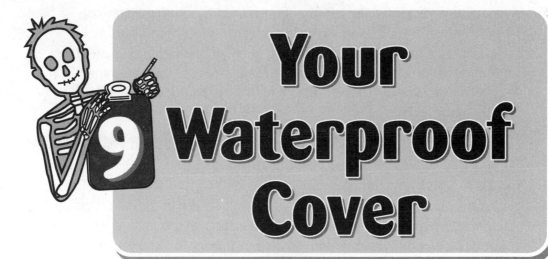

# Your Waterproof Cover

## The Skin

You have several characteristics in common with all other mammals. You are warm-blooded and have skin covered with hair. Your skin also has sweat glands. **Sweat glands** are curly-shaped glands located deep in the skin that produce sweat. Hair and sweat glands help mammals control their body temperature. Your skin also does many other things for you.

Skin forms a protective barrier against germs, infection, and general wear and tear. It also protects you from harmful ultraviolet (UV) rays from the sun. It keeps the body waterproof by keeping water from the outside from getting in and stopping fluids inside the body from being lost. It helps keep the body's internal temperature at a constant 98.6°F (37°C) by means of sweating and shivering. It contains the touch receptors, which are part of the nervous system.

To learn more about your skin, try the activities in this chapter.

## PROJECT 1 — SWEATING IT OUT

One important job that your skin does is to help keep your body at a constant temperature. The sweat glands in your skin help do this. Try this activity to learn more about how your sweat glands work.

### Materials

water

### Procedure

1. Blow on the inside of your forearm. How does your skin feel?

2. Place a few drops of water on the inside of your forearm and rub it into a small circle.

3. Blow on the wet circle. Does your skin feel different than when you blew on it without water?

## Explanation

When you blow on your wet forearm, you will notice that your skin seems cooler than when you blow on it when it is dry.

One way that your body controls its temperature is with sweat. Sweat is a salty liquid produced in curly-shaped sweat glands located deep in the skin. Sweat oozes to the skin's surface through tiny holes called **pores.** As sweat reaches the surface, it evaporates, or dries. As it does this, sweat draws warmth away from the skin and the area feels cooler. This helps cool down the body.

Your body has over 3 million sweat glands. Even on a cool day, you lose 0.5 pints (0.3 liters) of sweat. On a hot day, you can lose up to 3.5 pints (2 liters) of sweat.

 ## BLISTERS

Imagine that you touch the bottom of a pot that has been on a hot stove. You quickly pull your hand away, but it's too late. You've burned your finger and a blister begins to form. To learn more about blisters without getting burned, try this activity.

## Materials

red food coloring

measuring spoons

petroleum jelly

plate

yellow food coloring

toothpick

tissue paper

## Procedure

1. Place a drop of red food coloring on the back of your hand. Smear the drop to make a spot about the size of a quarter.

2. Place 1 teaspoon (5 ml) of petroleum jelly on the plate.

3. Add a drop of yellow food coloring to the petroleum jelly and mix with the toothpick.

4. Place the yellow mixture on top of the red spot on your hand so that it just covers it, making a bubble shape.

5. Tear off a piece of tissue paper that is just larger than the yellow blob on your hand. Lay the paper over the blob and gently push it into the mixture so that it sticks.

6. Cover the tissue paper with a thin layer of petroleum jelly and smooth it. The paper should become transparent.

7. After you have made your fake blister, go up to your brother or sister and ask him or her to help you "pop" your blister.

## Explanation

You have created a fake blister. If your skin comes into contact with something very hot, such as when you touch a hot pot, or if your skin is exposed to heat for a long time, such as when you stay in the sun too long, your skin can be damaged. Often damaged skin will form a blister. The petroleum jelly in this project acts like the fluid in a blister and the tissue paper acts like the outer layer of skin.

A **blister** is a raised patch of skin filled with a watery substance. Blisters are usually caused by heat, frostbite, or rubbing. The outer layer of your skin, the **epidermis,** covers the inner layer, the **dermis.** The dermis contains blood vessels, sweat glands, hair roots, and new skin cells. When skin cells are damaged by heat, such as when you touch a hot pot, fluid flows into the area to try to cool the area and collects between the dermis and the epidermis. This causes the epidermis to puff up. The fluid is mainly plasma, the liquid part of blood. The blister will remain until your body repairs the skin. Then the blister pops itself and/or dries up.

## HAIR BALL

Hair is another thing that makes us unique. Microscopic examination of hair can tell a lot about the person it came from, such as age, sex, and race. Try this activity to learn more about hair.

## Materials

strands of hair from several
   people or animals
transparent tape
several sheets of white paper
marker

magnifying lens
microscope (optional)
pencil
paper

## Procedure

1. Obtain strands of hair from several people. You can take some from a hairbrush, or cut or pull, *with permission,* several hairs from their heads. Include pet hairs in your investigation, if possible.

2. Tape each piece of hair on a separate sheet of white paper. With the marker, label whom the hair came from and how it was obtained.

3. Examine each hair with the magnifying lens and microscope, if available. Record your observations.

Ask a helper to obtain another piece of hair from someone who already gave you a hair sample. Using your sheets of paper and magnifying lens or microscope, can you identify whom the hair came from?

## Explanation

You should notice several differences between hairs from different people and between human hair and animal hair. These differences can include color, thickness, length, and so on.

You have about 5 million hairs on your body, of which about 100,000 are on your head. Hair grows out of deep pits in your skin called **follicles.** Cells at the base of hair divide and push the

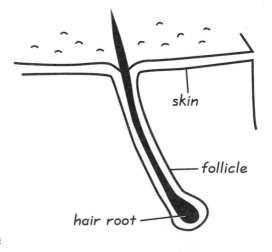

skin

follicle

hair root

hair up through the follicle. The hair you can see is made of dead cells, filled with the protein **keratin** and the brown pigment **melanin.** The more melanin your hair has, the darker it will be.

The first step in any examination of hair is to determine whether it is human hair. This is done by comparing the hair to known human samples. The next step is to note the features of the hair, such as the length, diameter, and color, including the distribution of color (hair may be lighter colored on one end) and any evidence of dyeing or bleaching.

Hair that has been pulled from the scalp—as opposed to hair that has been cut off, broken off, or has naturally fallen out—will often have tissue sticking to the **root** (the enlarged part of the hair, normally located below the skin).

Your hair grows about 0.08 inches (2 mm) a week. After about 2 or 3 years, hair stops growing and falls out. The follicle then rests for about 3 months, then produces a new hair. You lose about 70 hairs every day.

# MAKIN' MARKS

The skin on the tips of your fingers is covered with tiny ridges. These ridges are what make a fingerprint on surfaces you touch. Your fingerprints are very special. No two people, even identical twins, ever have exactly the same fingerprints. The first step in understanding fingerprints and fingerprinting is to examine your own.

## Materials

magnifying lens
pencil
2 sheets of white paper
transparent tape
marker
helper

## Procedure

1. Look at the ridges on your fingers through the magnifying lens.

2. Rub the pencil point back and forth many times on a sheet of white paper to make a small dark area of pencil lead dust.

3. Press one finger at a time into the dust. You may need to rub the pencil point again to get more dust for each fingerprint. Press all fingers of both hands into the dust.

4. Have your helper place the sticky side of a piece of tape on each dust-covered finger.

5. Stick each tape print on the other, clean sheet of white paper.

6. Use the marker to label each print with which finger and hand it came from.

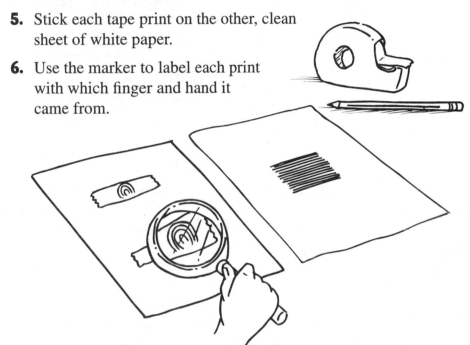

**More Fun Stuff to Do**

Create a complete set of fingerprints for several helpers. Use one sheet of paper for each set and label each print so that you know which finger and which person they came from. Next, have each helper make a fingerprint on a separate sheet of paper. Do not label these prints. Choose one of the unlabeled prints at random. Using your labeled sets of fingerprints, try to discover whose fingerprint it is. What can you do to make the task easier?

## Explanation

The skin on the palms of human hands (and the bottoms of our feet) is covered with tiny ridges, called **friction ridges.** These ridges allow people to pick up and handle objects easily. Each person has a totally unique pattern of ridges on his or her hands and feet. And for each person, the pattern on each finger or toe is unique and different from the pattern on any other finger or toe.

A **fingerprint** is the image of these ridge patterns transferred to a surface. Fingerprints occur because glands in your hands and feet secrete liquids, mainly sweat and oils. These liquids leave the patterned mark of your fingerprints on almost everything you touch.

## SMELLY FEET

Your body carries organisms that are too small to see without a microscope. These tiny creatures, called **microbes,** perform many tasks for you. Try this activity to discover some of these microbes and where they are found.

## Materials

| | |
|---|---|
| ½ cup (125 ml) water | tennis shoes |
| cooking pan | cotton swab |
| 4 packages of unflavored gelatin | rubber gloves |
| timer | adult helper |
| 1-quart (1-liter) jar with lid | |

## Procedure

1. Have your adult helper prepare the gelatin by boiling the water in the pan and dissolving the gelatin packages in the boiling water.

2. Allow the gelatin to cool until it is cool enough to handle but not solid (about 5 minutes).

3. When the gelatin has cooled, pour it into the jar.

4. Hold the jar over a trash can and tip the jar flat on its side to let the extra gelatin pour out.

5. Set the jar on its side and leave it undisturbed for 4 hours.

6. Put your tennis shoes on without socks and go play outside.

7. Remove your shoes. Take the cotton swab and rub it between all your toes.

8. Reach into the jar and carefully brush the gelatin with the cotton swab. Make a wavy line in the gelatin as shown.

9. Place the lid on the jar and put the jar on its side in a warm, dark location. Leave it there for 4 days.

10. Wash your hands and feet.

11. After the 4 days, observe the gelatin in the jar. What do you see? *CAUTION: Do not touch the gelatin because many microbes can cause disease!* Don't keep the jar longer than 4 days to keep the microbes from multiplying too much. When you are done with the experiment, put on rubber gloves, fill the jar with hot water, let it soak for 5 minutes, and then wash the jar. The gelatin will dissolve and can be washed down the sink. Be sure to wash your hands when you are finished.

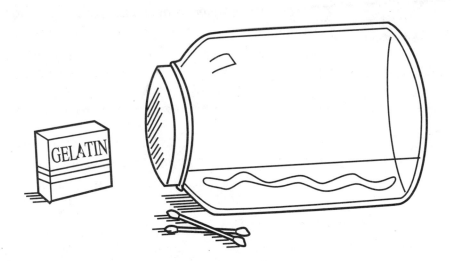

## Explanation

After a few days you will begin to see grooves, places where the gelatin has been eaten by microbes.

But where do the microbes come from? Do they come from your smelly feet? No, the real culprit of smelly feet is not so much your feet as it is your shoes. Feet sweat like other parts of your body. In addition, dead skin cells fall off them. Microbes, like bacteria and fungi, like to live is this environment. The inside of your shoes is dark, warm, and damp from sweat. This is a perfect environment for microbes to grow, since they are naturally attracted to warm, dark, damp places. Your jar has a similar environment. The gelatin provides food and a nice place to live for the microbes, so they eat and reproduce. But the waste they produce is what gives sweaty tennis shoes that terrific smell.

Microbes can also be found just about everywhere on and around your body, on skin and eyelashes, in dirt, and on the soles of shoes.

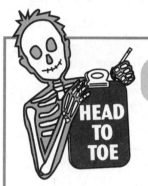

## SCIENCE IN ACTION

Forensic scientists compare microbes in a shoe found at a crime scene to known microbes and microbes found on a suspect. If the microbes match, they can be used to place the suspect at the crime scene.

# Glossary

**acid**   A substance that tastes sour and neutralizes bases.

**alveoli**   The small air sacs in the lungs where oxygen from the air is transferred into the blood and carbon dioxide is removed.

**amplify**   To make louder.

**antibody**   A special protein that is produced in response to a foreign substance in the blood.

**antigens**   Markers on red blood cells that identify blood type.

**anvil**   An anvil-shaped bone in the middle ear that amplifies sound.

**aorta**   The large blood vessel that leaves the heart.

**arteries**   Blood vessels that carry blood away from the heart. They have thick, elastic walls that can stretch with the rush of blood that comes with each heartbeat.

**auditory canal**   The section of the outer ear that connects and directs sound vibrations to the middle ear and inner ear. Also called the **ear canal.**

**auditory nerve**   The nerve that carries sound information as impulses from the ear to the brain.

**base**   A substance that tastes bitter and neutralizes acids.

**blister**   A raised patch of skin filled with plasma, usually caused by heat, frostbite, or rubbing.

**blood transfusion**   Removing blood from one person and giving it to another.

**bolus**   A lump of food that is swallowed.

**bone marrow**   The tissue inside bones that makes blood cells and stores fat.

**brain**   A collection of **interneurons** located in the head which link and control nerves within the body.

**bromothymol blue**   An acid indicator that will turn blue in a basic or neutral solution and green or yellow-green in an acidic solution.

**bronchial tubes**   Two tubes that lead from the trachea to the lungs.

**bronchioles**   Small branches of the bronchial tubes that are in the lungs and that attach to the alveoli.

**calcium**   An important mineral in the body that makes bones strong.

**capillaries**   The smallest blood vessels in the body. They are composed of a single layer of cells that travels next to the body's cells.

**carbonic acid**   A weak acid formed when carbon dioxide mixes with water.

**cardiac muscles**   Muscles that cause the heart to pump blood.

**cartilage**   Tough, fibrous tissue from which bone develops. It also covers the ends of some bones at joint areas.

**center of gravity**   The place where the effect of gravity seems to be concentrated.

**cervical vertebrae**   The seven neck bones of the spine.

**cilia**   Small hairs found on ciliated cells.

**circulatory system**   The system in the body that carries nutrients and oxygen to the cells and carries waste away. The blood, heart, and blood vessels make up the circulatory system.

**cochlea**   A fluid-filled chamber of the inner ear containing specialized hair cells that respond to sound waves of different vibrations.

**codon**   A code found on DNA consisting of three nucleic acids in a row on the DNA strand.

**compact bone**   Bone that is composed of hard, dense materials, such as the leg bone.

**consolidation time**   The time needed for new memory of information or a task to be stored in a permanent, chemical way.

**cornea**   A thin, clear disk that covers the eye to protect it.

**deciduous teeth**   The first set of teeth, which begins to appear in babies.

**dermis**   The inner layer of skin.

**diaphragm**   A band of muscles located at the bottom of the chest cavity that contracts and relaxes during inhalation and exhalation.

**digestive system**   The system of the body responsible for breaking down large, complex food molecules into small components that can be absorbed and used by the body.

**DNA (deoxyribonucleic acid)**   The only known chemical that can reproduce itself.

**dominant**   Relating to a trait that does produce physical characteristics.

**dominant eye**   The favored eye, which usually sees an object slightly better than the nondominant eye.

**ear canal**   See **auditory canal.**

**eardrum**   The section of the middle ear that vibrates when sound vibrations hit it, causing the hammer, anvil, and stirrup to vibrate as well.

**egg**   The female reproductive cell.

**electrochemical impulse**   A process that uses chemicals to create an electrical impulse.

**endoskeleton**   A skeleton located on the inside of the body. Humans have this type of skeleton.

**enzyme**   A special chemical that makes chemical reactions happen faster.

**epidermis**   The outer layer of skin.

**esophagus**   A tube that connects the mouth to the stomach.

**eustachian tube**   The tube that connects the middle ear to the mouth and nose.

**exoskeleton**   A skeleton located on the outside of the body. Insects have this type of skeleton.

**farsightedness**   See **hyperopia.**

**fatigue**   Tiredness that occurs when a muscle's ability to function decreases because of repeated contractions.

**femur**   The upper leg bone.

**fertilization**   The process by which an egg and a sperm come together to start a new organism.

**fibula**   One of two lower leg bones.

**fingerprint**   The image of a finger's friction ridge patterns transferred to a surface.

**flexible**   Able to bend.

**follicle**   A deep pit in the dermis that hairs grow out of.

**friction ridges**   Tiny ridges found on the palms of human hands and the bottom of human feet.

**gene**   The part of a chromosome that produces a specific trait in an individual.

**genetics**   The study of heredity, the passing of traits from parents to children.

**gluteus maximus**   The muscles in the buttocks, which are connected to the back of the thighs.

**hammer**   A hammer-shaped bone in the middle ear that amplifies sound.

**horsepower**   A unit of power. One unit of horsepower (hp) is equal to 746 watts.

**humerus**   The upper arm bone.

**hyperopia**   A condition that occurs when the muscles of the eye cannot make the lens thick enough to produce a clear image on the retina. Commonly called **farsightedness.** Someone who is farsighted is able to focus on distant objects but has trouble seeing objects that are close.

**hypothesis**   An educated guess about the results of an experiment to be performed.

**inertia**   The tendency of an object to remain at rest or continue moving unless acted on by an outside force.

**inner ear**   The inner section of the ear, composed of the **semicircular canals,** the **cochlea,** and the **auditory nerve.**

**interneuron**   A nerve that links other nerves within the body.

**involuntary muscles**   Muscles, like the muscles of the heart and digestive system, that work on their own, without help.

**iodine**   A chemical that turns dark blue or black when it reacts with starch.

**iris**   The colored area around the pupil of the eye, which automatically regulates the amount of light entering the eye.

**joint**   A place where two or more bones come together.

**keratin**   A protein found in hair and fingernails.

**lens**   A piece of glass or other transparent substance with a curved surface that refracts light rays passing through it. The part of the eye that is just inside the pupil and operates much like a camera lens or magnifying lens by refracting light rays to meet at the retina.

**lumbar vertebrae**   The five lower back bones of the spine.

**melanin**   A brown pigment that gives hair and skin its color.

**microbes**   Tiny organisms that can be seen only with a microscope.

**middle ear**   The middle section of the ear, composed of the **eardrum, the hammer, the anvil, the stirrup,** and the **eustachian tube.**

**mineral**   A nonliving, naturally occurring substance.

**motor cortex**   The area of the brain responsible for creating and sending the messages that cause movement.

**motor nerves**   Nerves that direct muscles to move.

**mucus**   A substance that lines the entire digestive and respiratory tracts. Mucus protects the lining of the digestive tract and is slippery to allow the food to move more easily. It is also slightly sticky and is used in the respiratory tract to help clean air before it enters the lungs.

**myopia**   A condition that occurs when the muscles of the eye cannot make the lens thin enough to produce a clear image on the retina. Commonly called **nearsightedness.** Someone who is nearsighted is able to focus on close objects but has difficulty seeing objects that are far away.

**nearsightedness**   See **myopia.**

**nerves**   Special cells with long extensions that communicate using electrochemical impulses.

**nervous system**   The parts of the body that control the physical reactions to the environment. The nervous system consists of the brain, spinal cord, and nerves.

**neutral**   Neither acidic nor basic.

**newton**   A unit of force.

**nucleic acids**   Four chemical messengers in DNA: adenine, guanine, thymine, and cytosine.

**olfactory nerve**   The nerve that carries smell information as impulses from either side of the nose to the brain.

**optic nerve**   The nerve that carries visual information as impulses from the eye to the brain.

**optical illusion**   A picture or image that results in a false impression.

**organisms**   Living things.

**outer ear**   The outer section of the ear, composed of the **pinna** and the **auditory canal.**

**papillae**   The small bumps on the surface of the tongue where the **taste buds** are located.

**pelvis**   The bones that make up the hips.

**periosteum**   A thin covering on the outside of bone, containing blood vessels, nerves, and bone-forming cells.

**peristalsis**   The movement of food through the digestive system by means of rhythmic, wavelike contractions of the muscles lining the digestive tract.

**permanent teeth**   The second set of teeth, which replaces the deciduous teeth between the ages of 6 and 18.

**pinna**   The outer ear flap, which collects sound.

**plasma**   The liquid part of blood that is mainly salt water.

**platelets**   Blood cells that help the blood to clot and form scabs so that cuts heal.

**pores**   Tiny holes in the skin.

**pupil**   The small black spot in the middle of the eye, which acts as an opening that allows light to enter.

**radius**   One of two bones of the forearm.

**reaction time**   The amount of time it takes for a message to travel from the brain to the muscles in the body and cause a movement.

**recessive**   Relating to a trait that does not produce physical characteristics.

**red blood cells**   Blood cells that carry oxygen to body cells and carry carbon dioxide away.

**refract**   What light does when it bends, as when a lens bends and brings together rays of light passing through it.

**respiratory system**   The system of the body involved in breathing.

**retina**   The part of the eye where light rays meet and which records the image and transfers it to the brain through the optic nerve.

**ribs**   The bones that enclose the chest cavity.

**root**   The enlarged part of the hair, normally located below the skin.

**saliva**   An enzyme that is secreted from the salivary glands and mixes with food to speed the digestion of starch.

**scientific method**   The process used to investigate a scientific question that involves forming a hypothesis, testing the hypothesis with an experiment, analyzing the results, and drawing a conclusion.

**semicircular canals**   Three loop-shaped tubular structures in the inner ear that help the body maintain balance.

**sensory nerves**  Nerves that collect information from the environment such as heat, cold, touch, pressure, and pain.

**skeletal muscles**  Muscles that help you move.

**smooth muscles**  Muscles that help you to swallow, control the movement of food along your digestive system, and are involved in the operation of your internal organs.

**sound**  Energy that can be heard.

**sperm**  The male reproductive cell.

**spinal cord**  A collection of **interneurons** running through the backbone that carries information from **sensory nerves** to the **brain** and from the **brain** to **motor nerves.**

**spongy bone**  Bone that is made up of lighter, less dense materials, such as the ribs.

**starch**  A large molecule made up of many smaller sugar molecules linked together.

**stirrup**  A stirrup-shaped bone in the middle ear that amplifies sound.

**stroke volume**  The amount of blood the heart pumps with each beat.

**sweat glands**  Curly-shaped glands located deep in the skin that produce a salty liquid to help control body temperature.

**synapse**  A small gap where the electrochemical impulse releases a chemical messenger that transfers the impulse from one nerve cell to the next.

**taste buds**  Taste receptors located on the small bumps on the surface of the tongue.

**tendon**  Strong tissue that connects muscle to bone.

**thoracic vertebrae**  The 12 upper back bones of the spine.

**tibia**  One of two lower leg bones.

**trachea**  A tube that leads from the mouth to the bronchial tubes. Commonly called the **windpipe.**

**ulna**  One of two bones of the forearm.

**veins**  Blood vessels that carry blood back to the heart. They have thin walls and one-way valves.

**vena cava**  The large vein that leads to the right side of the heart.

**vibrate**  To move back and forth very rapidly.

**voluntary muscles**  Muscles which are controlled consciously.

**watts**  A unit of power.

**white blood cells**  Blood cells that help the body fight infection and disease.

**windpipe**  See **trachea.**

**wisdom teeth**  The common name for the third set of molars, which appears at about age 18.

**zygote**  The first cell formed after a sperm and an egg combine.

# Index

lumbar vertebrae, 83, 85
lungs, 48–50, 51, 62

melanin, 106
memory, 12
Mendel, Gregor, 100
methane, 46
microbe growing, 108–10
middle ear, 26, 27
minerals, 38, 43, 81, 82, 87
molars, 39–40
motor cortex, 9
motor nerves, 6
movement, 9, 17, 19, 70
mucus, 45, 49, 55–56
muscles, 70–78
  circulatory system and, 59
  digestion and, 38, 45
  exercise and, 76, 82
  movement and, 9, 70
  respiration and, 53–54
myopia, 25

nearsightedness, 25
nervous system, 6–36
neutral solution, 51
newtons, 71–72
nitrogen, 48
nose, 29–30, 33–34, 49,
  55–56
nucleic acids, 98

oils (dietary), 43
olfactory nerve, 34
optical illusions, 12–14
optic nerve, 24
organisms, 6
outer ear, 26

oxygen
  blood and, 58–59, 61–67
  breathing and, 48, 50,
   54–55
  muscles and, 76, 78
  sensory nerves and, 22

papillae, 31
pelvis, 83, 85
periosteum, 88
peristalsis, 45
permanent teeth, 39–40
phosphorus, 87
pinna, 26, 27
plasma, 63, 64, 104
platelets, 63, 64
pores, 103
proteins, 38, 43
pulse, 60–61, 67
pupil (eye), 24

radius (bone), 84, 85
reaction time, 8–10
recessive genes, 93, 98–99
red blood cells, 55, 63, 64–65
refraction, 23
reproductive system, 92–100
respiratory system, 48–56
retina, 24, 25
ribs, 80, 83, 85
roots, hair, 105, 106

saliva, 31, 40–41
science fair projects, 2–3
scientific method, 3
semicircular canal, 19, 27
senses, 6, 22–36
sensory nerves, 6, 22
sight, 7–8, 12–17, 22–25